STUDENTS, TEACHERS, FAMILIES, AND A SOCIALLY JUST EDUCATION

Professor Julie Allan
and Dr Francesca Peruzzo

STUDENTS, TEACHERS, FAMILIES, AND A SOCIALLY JUST EDUCATION

Rewriting the Grammar of Schooling to Unsettle Identities

The Education
Studies Collection

Collection Editor
Dr Janise Hurtig

First published in 2023 by Lived Places Publishing.

All rights reserved. No part of this publication may be reproduced, stored in a retrieval system, or transmitted in any form or by any means, electronic, mechanical, photocopying, recording or otherwise, without prior permission in writing from the publisher.

The authors and editors have made every effort to ensure the accuracy of information contained in this publication, but assume no responsibility for any errors, inaccuracies, inconsistencies and omissions. Likewise, every effort has been made to contact copyright holders. If any copyright material has been reproduced unwittingly and without permission the Publisher will gladly receive information enabling them to rectify any error or omission in subsequent editions.

Copyright © 2023 Lived Places Publishing

British Library Cataloguing in Publication Data
A CIP record for this book is available from the British Library

ISBN: 9781915271754 (pbk)
ISBN: 9781915271778 (ePDF)
ISBN: 9781915271761 (ePUB)

The right of Julie Allan and Francesca Peruzzo to be identified as the Authors of this work has been asserted by them in accordance with the Copyright, Design and Patents Act 1988.

Cover design by Fiachra McCarthy

Book design by Rachel Trolove of Twin Trail Design
Typeset by Newgen Publishing UK

Lived Places Publishing
Long Island
New York 11789

www.livedplacespublishing.com

Abstract

Education has been and continues to be shaped, informed, and driven by a so-called "grammar of schooling": an approach which completely ignores the many and diverse identities that learners own, are given, and encounter. Categorising students into neat, labelled boxes; splintering knowledge into strictly defined subjects; and fracturing learning – this grammar of schooling desperately needs rewriting.

Through narratives from teachers, students, and students' families, this book explores the lived experiences of those who are forced to live with the current approach, and the consequences for their lives, relationships, and education. It also asks the question of what creative and holistic alternative approaches might look like.

Keywords

Diversity; equity; equality; inclusion; DEIB; social identity; lived experience; learning; creativity; accessibility

Contents

Learning objectives   viii

Chapter 1   Schooling, technologies, and equity in times of crisis   1

Chapter 2   The repetition of the grammar of schooling   27

Chapter 3   Rewriting the grammar of schooling   61

Chapter 4   Unsettling identities for a socially just inclusion?   95

References   122

Index   145

Learning objectives

1. To recognise the value of the lived experiences of education professionals.
2. To understand the idea of the "grammar of schooling" and its historical origins.
3. To recognise the impact of global dynamics on local realities.
4. To appreciate the impact of the COVID-19 pandemic, particularly on disadvantaged groups.
5. To understand the role of technologies in inclusive education.
6. To become aware of the possibilities for challenging the grammar of schooling.

1
Schooling, technologies, and equity in times of crisis

> The secret wish of us all, what we think about all the time, is when will it end? But it will not end: it is reasonable to see the ongoing pandemic as announcing a new era of ecological troubles.
>
> (Žižek, 2021, p. 12)

The impact of the COVID-19 pandemic has been, without doubt, a global catastrophe, "upending the lives of children and families" (UNICEF, 2020a) and providing an "existential threat to humanity and an equitable world" (Bardosh et al., 2019, p. 14). The pandemic has widened the gap between those already disadvantaged and others and created a "double jeopardy" (UNICEF, 2020b) for children living in poverty. It has also exposed some new, highly disadvantaged groups, including migrant workers, whom Stein, Latour, and Schultz (2019, p. 224) describe as part of the "geo-social classes". Žižek (2021, p. 20) points out that "this new working class was here all along, the pandemic just propelled it into visibility".

Education faced, as a result of the pandemic, "an emergency of unprecedented scale" (Reuge et al., 2021, p. 2). Schools were plunged into crisis mode, forced to close with little notice, and required to redirect and recreate learning for their students at home. According to UNICEF (2021), schools across the world were closed between March 2020 and February 2021 for an average of 95 instruction days, amounting to roughly half of what children should have had. Countries in Latin America and the Caribbean had the greatest number of closures (losing 158 days of instruction), followed by South Asian countries (closed for 146 days), and countries in Eastern and Southern Africa (with an average of 101 days of closure). UNICEF (2021) estimates that 214 million students globally have missed at least three quarters of classroom instruction time, with 168 million children from 14 countries missing almost all instruction time because of school closures.

Everyone will have their own story of where they were when they learned that we were entering a pandemic and about to go into lockdown. In the interests of stimulating readers to reflect on their own experiences, we recall ours. Julie was in the last few months as Head of the School of Education at the University of Birmingham in the UK as the news from the senior leaders at the regular Monday morning meetings was becoming increasingly bleak. We were being advised to prepare for imminent closure and to make arrangements for the conversion to online learning. Expert colleagues from the medical school added their gloomy prognoses and confirmed that the pandemic was going to be "catastrophic". Despite the consensus, Julie still couldn't quite believe that this was going to happen and as she relayed the news to the senior leaders in the School of Education, their reactions suggested they didn't quite believe it – or her – either. That was soon to change.

Francesca had recently finished her doctorate at the University College London, Institute of Education in London. Eager to contribute to make higher education a more inclusive and socially just institution for disabled students and for students from minority backgrounds, at the time, she was working as a special educational needs tutor for a local charity while publishing from her doctoral thesis and engaging with disabled student activists to bring change in higher education institutions in the UK. She remembers being on a bus on her way to the local charity when the lockdown was announced. Her thoughts went straight to her students, many of whom had multiple impairments and developmental disabilities who came from challenging family backgrounds. She wondered how the situation would impact their lives and education.

The COVID-19 pandemic has, without doubt, provoked a crisis in education, as elsewhere in public life. However, as many educationists and observers have been arguing for several years, education was in crisis long before the pandemic hit. Arendt (2006), for example, highlights the harm done to children by education through its failure to secure the vital conditions necessary for growth and development. Others (Ball and Collet-Sabé, 2021; Ladson-Billings, 2021; Darling-Hammond, 2001) have drawn attention to the huge and growing inequities, especially for minority ethnic groups, produced within a system that insists that "everyone do better than everyone else" (McDermott, 1993, p. 274).

This book is both a response to the COVID-19 pandemic, which of course remains with us, and to the wider, and more enduring, crisis in education. By sharing the lived experiences of professionals – through the pandemic and in their careers more generally – we uncover how specific educational spaces (the school and, during the pandemic, the home) are encountered and *lived*. We also, in turn, consider how these experiences shape individuals' identities. We reflect critically on how, within these educational spaces, some of the less educational aspects of schooling – what has been referred to as the "grammar of schooling" (Tyack and Tobin, 1994, p. 453; Zhao, 2020, p. 198) – are repeated, leading to the "repetition of exclusion" (Allan, 2006, p. 121):

> The grammar of schooling, such as standardized organizational practices in dividing time and space, classifying students and allocating them to classrooms, and splintering knowledge into 'subjects', is so powerful that it has persisted despite many repeated challenges by very courageous, intelligent, and powerful innovators. It has persisted despite mounting evidence and widespread acknowledgement that it is obsolete and does not serve our children well.
>
> (Zhao, 2020, p. 198)

In spite of the persistence of the grammar of schooling, which is revealed through the professionals' lived experiences, this is, nevertheless, an optimistic and hopeful book, and we also demonstrate, through the professionals, the possibilities for rewriting the grammar of schooling. We turn now to describe the project within which we obtained the lived experiences that we report in this book.

Lived DIGITAL experiences

The research that informs this book took place within a year-long project entitled *DIGITAL (Diversifying Inclusion and Growth: Inclusive Technologies for Accessible Learning) in a time of Coronavirus*. We investigated the role of digital and non-digital technologies in promoting inclusive practices during the COVID-19 pandemic response of countries in the Global North and South. Data were obtained through interviews with educators, teachers, headteachers, teaching assistants, and leaders of grassroots organisations in England, the US, Australia, Italy, Chile, and Malaysia. Since the project took place in the middle of the pandemic, all of the interviews were carried out online by Zoom. However, we were able to visit Malaysia when restrictions were lifted and see for ourselves the spaces – and the students and staff living and working in these spaces – that project participants had described. This may explain, in advance, any possible over-representation of the Malaysian context. It certainly reminds us of the power of the physical experience of space.

By creating moments for lived experiences of teachers to be heard, and by reading these in conjunction with key theoretical ideas, we have been able to understand more acutely the extent of the injustices, oppression, and disadvantage experienced in education. We were also able to understand how teachers' actions could improve the lives of their students and alter their identities as teachers, students, and communities. The key ideas that we used come from decolonial theory (De Lissovoy, 2010; Mignolo, 2011; Santos, 2018; 2021) and from conceptualisations by the philosophers Foucault (2004; 1977), especially his concept of epistemic grid and the relations between power and knowledge and dividing practices in education and Deleuze and Guattari (1987), in particular smooth and striated spaces, deterritorialisation, the rhizome, and lines of flight. We "use" theory here purely to help understand what is going on in the teachers' lived experiences and to explore the potential for making things better than they were before. We unpack these ideas, and how we used them, a little further below.

Decolonial theory assisted in our reading of the grammar of schooling and in drawing attention to:

> The production and validation of knowledges anchored in the experiences of resistance of all those groups that have systematically suffered injustices, oppression, and destruction caused by capitalism, colonialism and patriarchy.
>
> (Santos, 2018, p. 1)

Because decolonial theory draws attention to the structural and systemic origins of oppression, we were able to explore how some of these oppressions get translated within school and curriculum, without laying any blame on the teachers. Foucault's epistemic grid helped us to problematise and interrogate the way in which these practices become routinised, ingrained and naturalised. Decolonial theory further helped us to recognise the potential of some of the teachers' actions in altering the curriculum to bring forth new, alternative knowledges that could alter the students' subjectivities.

Deleuze and Guattari's (1987) conceptualisation of smooth and striated spaces also assisted in the understanding of the closures created within the grammar of schooling and the nature of the spaces in which it operates. The chief function of the state, according to Deleuze and Guattari (1987), is to create striations in the spaces of institutions, including schools, that help to control and contain individuals. Within smooth spaces, on the other hand, "life reconstitutes its stakes, confronts new obstacles, invents new paces, switches adversaries" (Deleuze and Guattari, 1987, p. 500). Deleuze and Guattari offered an encouragement to create smooth spaces, which they described as deterritorialisation. This, to them, was opportunistic rather than strategic and required invention and creativity. Having these ideas in our mind as we encountered the teachers' lived experiences, we were able to recognise some of their actions as deliberately working on the spaces of the school and the curriculum and changing them for the better.

The rhizome was introduced by Deleuze and Guattari (1987) as both a concept and a model of thought to provide an alternative way of thinking about knowledge and about the means of acquiring that knowledge. Conventional knowledge, according to Deleuze and Guattari (1987), is rigid, striated, and hierarchical, with a tree-like structure, and learning involves merely a transfer of knowledge (from the teacher to the student) in a process "which articulates and hierarchizes tracings" (Deleuze and Guattari, 1987, p. 12). The rhizome (real-life examples of which are ginger and snake plants), in contrast, moves in messy and unpredictable ways; has multiple connections, lines, and points of rupture; and "releases us from the false bondage of linear relationships" (Roy, 2003, p. 90). The rhizome offers possibilities for rewriting the grammar of schooling in new, creative ways and we were able to recognise children's learning, depicted by their teachers, as having rhizomic properties. We also understood the children's learning as following new lines of flight, with literally new directions and new knowledges formed within and through these lines. This kind of learning seemed to offer promise for undoing the grammar of schooling and replacing it with new, smoother alternatives:

> This is how it should be done: Lodge yourself on a stratum; experiment with the opportunities it offers, find an advantageous place on it, find potential movements of deterritorialization, possible lines of flight, experience them, produce flow conjunctions here and there, try out continuums of intensities segment by segment, have a small plot of new land at all times.
> (Deleuze and Guattari, 1987, p. 161)

These theoretical resources are extremely useful in understanding how and why the grammar of schooling continues to endure and in appreciating the extent of its damage. They are also crucial in helping us to imagine how things might be done differently. But it was the participants in our project, the teachers, school leaders, parents and heads of governmental and non-governmental organisations, who inspired us to believe in the possibility of rewriting the grammar of schooling – by doing that rewriting themselves. We turn, for the remainder of this chapter, to some critical reflections on three key elements of the study: schools and schooling, technologies, and equity. Schools and schooling were central to the study as the main arena in which the grammar of schooling operated; technologies were at the heart of every country's response to the pandemic, supporting the switch to learning at home; equity, and of course inequity, is a crucial element of the impact of the pandemic responses and of the grammar of schooling before that.

Schooling

Concerns by governments, and by the public, about what students were losing out on by not being in school became converted into significant panic about "loss of learning" (Roberts and Danechi, 2022). However, as Bello (2021) points out, the notion of learning loss is merely a marketing catchphrase intended to bring financial benefits to publishers of tests and financial consultants. Nevertheless, fears about learning loss led to the commissioning of two reports on this topic from the UK-based Education Policy Institute (EPI, 2020a and b) and a study by the assessment company Renaissance Learning (also UK in origin but with a global reach) which used its own school testing software (Burrows, 2021; Williamson, Macgilchrist, and Potter, 2021). EPI (2020a and b) established that learning losses in primary school were 3.7 months in mathematics and 1.2 months in reading by the first half of the autumn term of 2020. These had reduced by the second half of that term to 2.7 months for mathematics, although reading remained at 1.2 months. By the second half of the spring term, in March 2021 and after the second lockdown, learning losses had increased again to 3.5 months in mathematics and 2.2 months in reading. The findings of the Renaissance study, showing significant learning loss, were published by the Department for Education (GOV.UK, 2021) and Williamson, Macgilchrist, and Potter (2021) note that Renaissance happens to also supply projects for mitigation of learning gaps through programmes of accelerated learning and personalised learning plans (www.renlearn.co.uk/star-asse ssments/). Governments made available a range of measures to enable children to catch up; these included the Renaissance acceleration programmes, tutor-led programmes in mathematics and English, summer schools, and extensions to the school day. UNICEF (2020c), the World Bank, and the United Nations Refugee Agency all endorsed fully the principles and benefits of accelerated education. However, some critics considered the measures put in place to be "too late" for the pupils in greatest need (Ferguson, 2020).

Reay (2020, p. 311) argues that the pandemic has accentuated "two seismic fault lines" in English education, with one coming to have precedence over the other. She suggests that one fault line, that sees education as having inherent value in and of itself, is gradually being eroded in favour of a view of education as merely a means to economic and productive ends. Reay argues that the economic imperative has been driven by a government desperate to restart the economy and fearful that children will no longer be fit to support the economy and drive the country's recovery. Whilst Reay's argument is compelling, our view is that the problem goes much deeper and lies in a fixation with schooling and what goes on in schools rather than with education, leading to schools becoming sites of "division, exclusion, normalisation, and categorisation" (Ball and Collet-Sabé, 2021, p. 3). This situation of dysfunctional and damaging schooling has little to do with the teachers' practices or professionalism and everything to do with the way schools are forced to operate to sort and select, to channel and organise students, and to ensure lines of accountability are prioritised and adhered to. Ball and Collet-

Sabé (2021, p. 1) conclude that schools have become "intolerable" institutions. We remain much more optimistic that schools can become more focused on educating than on schooling children. We are, however, concerned about the ease with which schools, in their role of *loco parentis* and entrusted with responsibilities in relation to children, assume full control over the bodies and minds of the children and young people in their charge (Allan and Harwood, 2022).

Schools are highly structured organisations that are intensively scrutinised and subjected to regimes of accountability. The low levels of trust that ensue create tensions (2103) relating to performativity, with increasing pressures upon teachers. The "centre" (governments and municipalities) and its demands create fear for teachers and school leaders:

> Work in many schools is dominated by a continuous fear of inspection and an obsession with meeting centrally set targets so that the balance of the curriculum is disrupted and education can become the incessant process of preparing for the tests and being tested.
>
> (Booth, 2003, p. 36)

Elliot (2001, p. 202) suggests that the auditing and accountability processes visited upon schools creates a kind of "colonisation" that leads to "pathologies of creative compliance in the form of gamesmanship around an indicator culture". In other words, they force school leaders and teachers to concentrate on how well they are seen to be doing against a set of indicators, amidst a "tyranny of transparency" (Strathern, 2000, p. 309). Furthermore, they lead to the adoption of policies of equality that ensure the same for all, rather than equity, providing differentially for each individual. As we discuss later in this chapter, the emphasis on equality creates significant disadvantages for selected groups.

The space of the school that the child or young person encounters is both "sedentary" (Deleuze and Guattari, 1987, p. 474), requiring passivity from them, and "impossibly circumscribed" (Roy, 2003, p. 82). Schools operate along striated lines, even to the extent of compelling students to follow the lines and arrows depicting a one-way system. A series of "order words" (Deleuze and Parnett, 1987, p. 22) restricts their senses and forces them to respond to the sounds that dominate the school space. The most audible of these are the recurrent bell (or more modern equivalents), signalling a change of class and activity, and the teacher's constant verbosity:

> Teachers declaim, explain, clarify, define and preach endlessly. They flit from one thought to another, slip in a cherished question, repeat the elicited answer, nod the head, point the finger, make all manner of movements, and so on and so forth.
>
> (Depaepe et al., 2000, p. 77)

The dominance of the auditory blocks out other sensations for the students and leaves little room for how they *feel*.

Technologies

The technologies that are moving towards the digitalisation of our lives (Žižek, 2021) have generated both suspicion and intrigue in equal measure. On the one hand, there are concerns about the incremental "surveillance capitalism" (Žižek, 2021, p. 13) exercised upon us by state and private organisations and used in the governance of individuals and populations: "The subjectivities nurtured by these techniques of governance are frequently not those of choosing individuals" (Johns, 2021, p. 53). On the other hand, there is hope and curiosity about the potential of brain-related technologies, including the "wired brain" (Žižek, 2021, p. 13) and artificial intelligence, to enhance lives with minimal effort (Southgate, 2021). Wyatt-Smith, Lingard, and Heck (2021, p. 2) introduced the phrase "digital disruption" to capture the ambivalent ways in which technologies have penetrated teaching and testing in education, signalling that "a great technological and data juggernaut" (Lingard, Wyatt-Smith, and Heck, 2021, p. 4) has been released and is gaining increasing control over individuals' lives and futures. Three possibilities for what these futures might entail for the student subject are offered by Macgilchrist, Allert, and Bruch (2020). These are the "smooth users, competent subjects" (p. 77) whose access and use has increased through data analytics and artificial intelligence and who are expected to fit in seamlessly to the digital future created for them: "digital nomads, exploiting digitalisation for individualism" (p. 80) and increased mobility, whereby schools and schooling become superfluous; and "collective agents, in institutions as spaces for exploring new forms of living" (p. 82). It is possible to envisage each of these student subject futures becoming reality, although the "smooth user, competent subject" remains the most likely in the absence of any individual activism or community engagement.

In 2021, the United Nations recognised children's rights to access technologies (and to be protected from them) by endorsing General Comment No. 25 on children's rights in the context of a digital environment (UNCRC, 2021):

> The rights of every child must be respected, protected and fulfilled in the digital environment. Innovations in digital technologies affect children's lives and their rights in ways that are wide-ranging and interdependent, even where children do not themselves access the Internet.

Pangrazio and Sefton-Green (2021) argue that the word "digital" is usually an unnecessary adjective, but when placed in front of "rights", "citizenship", and "literacy", it "exerts a normative effect" (p. 17). This is achieved by presuming progress, increased scale and size, changes in human dimensions, and new norms and expectations, and precipitate, Pangrazio and Sefton-Green suggest, new forms of governance, control, and accountability. Williamson, Macgilchrist, and Potter (2021, p. 117) have observed the "disruptive and transformative force" of educational technologies on education systems across the globe. They attribute much of this to market influences and the return sought by investors as they attempt to transform education. Although there is consensus about the transformative potential of technologies for education, there is also recognition that they can expose children to harm (UNCRC, 2021; Williamson, Macgilchrist, and Potter, 2021). Meaningful digital access can enable children to realise civil, political, cultural, economic, and social rights, but it can also lead to the denial of these rights if digital inclusion is not enacted (UNCRC, 2021).

Illich (2009) has identified the negative consequences arising from a misplaced belief in technologies as a remedy for crises – realised through mere escalation. Instead of resolving the crises and associated problems, more information, datasets, and management systems are demanded and supplied (see also Selwyn, 2017). Technologies and tools are recruited to work for people (even though they often create obligations and constraints) rather than being designed for people to work with and Illich calls for technologies and tools to have a degree of "conviviality" (Illich, 2009, p. 11) to ensure freedom for individuals:

> I chose the term 'conviviality' to designate the opposite of industrial productivity. I intend it to mean autonomous and creative intercourse among persons, and the intercourse of persons with their environment; and this in contrast with the conditioned response to the demands made upon them by others, and by a man-made environment. I consider conviviality to be individual freedom realised in personal interdependence and, as such, an intrinsic ethical value.
> (Illich, 2009, p. 11)

Whilst it is claimed that technologies can foster greater equity in education through the increased accessibility of learning opportunities and the enhanced learning effectiveness for those with greatest need (Selwyn and Jandrić, 2020), it is also acknowledged that achievement gaps can remain unchanged or even widened by a lack of access to devices or to connectivity (Selwyn and Jandrić, 2020; Southgate, 2021). Learning analytics, used to design systems to detect students at risk of drop out, and personalised learning programmes that help maintain student engagement (Murphy et al., 2020), as Bello (2021) reminds us, generate profits for the private companies behind them.

When the COVID-19 pandemic hit, forcing widespread school closure and the shift to learning at home, attention turned to technologies and how they might support students' learning. The impact of missing school was anticipated as much as it was actually experienced, and this is because, through the "growing pretensions of school" (Illich, 2009, p. 64), physical, in-person attendance has become valorised more than the learning that takes place when the students are there. The pandemic, in denying students access to schools and schooling, exposed their two-fold purpose:

> not only to grade people for jobs but to upgrade them for consumption. As industrial output rises, it pushes the education system to exercise the social control necessary for its efficient use.
>
> (Illich, 2009, p. 62)

The huge expansion of networks, public-private partnerships, and government-financed outsourced contracts provided emergency technological solutions – to schools and in support of home learning – but also began to lay the ground for more permanent forms of engagement with technologies (Williamson and Hogan, 2020; Peruzzo, Ball, and Grimaldi, 2022).

The effects of the relocation of learning to the home have been felt differentially, with some finding it horrid, oppressive, and stressful, while others have enjoyed some of the freedoms afforded by the new home-based learning environment (Gourley et al., 2021; Williamson, Macgilchrist, and Potter; 2021; Watermeyer et al., 2021). It is not only the teachers who have such mixed experiences; students have also encountered learning at home and online in different ways and with different degrees of success. There are many stories of success in the ways in which technologies have been used to engage learners at home, many of them involving play and creativity (Corona Showcase, 2021; Pandemic Play Project, 2022; Williamson, Macgilchrist, and Potter, 2021). There have also been many instances of schools adapting quickly and efficiently to online learning and succeeding in supporting all learners at home. Indeed, we will share some of the success stories that we uncovered in Chapter 3. It is clear, however, that access to technologies, in the form of devices and connectivity and support to develop the skills to engage effectively with the technologies, has been uneven and inequitable. The digital divide (Starr, Hayes, and Gao, 2022; Gorski, 2005) can be said to be operating at three levels: the first and most basic level is access to the Internet; the second level involves inequalities in use, skills, and purposes of the use of technology; at the third level there are uneven opportunities for individuals to improve their life chances by reinvesting the resources and knowledge they have acquired online (Ragnedda and Muschert, 2018). The digital divide has had a profoundly detrimental impact on black and minority students and students from disadvantaged backgrounds. Students with special needs have also been adversely affected as a result of the inaccessibility of some technologies (Bradley, 2021). An increased role of businesses in education, leading to new forms of network governance and heterarchical relations (Peruzzo, Ball, and Grimaldi, 2022, see also Ball, 2012), has sought to reduce the digital divide. There is little evidence of success so far, and there have been significant problems in the supply and functioning of appropriate technologies to children and families (Good Law Project, 2021). At the same time, there have been huge financial gains for the private sector (Carr, 2021; Williamson, Macgilchrist, and Potter, 2021). Furthermore, technology companies have gained a stronger foothold through what Mollicchi et al. (2020, p. 279) call "resilient, infrastructural forms of dominance". This has raised concerns, once again, about the impact of the involvement of the private sector in public education (Teräs et al., 2020; Lingard, Wyatt-Smith, and Heck, 2021).

Equity

There have been many calls, over recent years, for the privileging of equity over equality in society. Equality means giving everyone the same thing, and equity is giving everyone whatever they need to succeed. As an anonymous source quoted by RISE (Research on Improving Systems of Education) puts it, "equality is giving everyone a pair of shoes. Equity is giving everyone a pair of shoes that fit". However, both equality and equity are underpinned by principles of fairness and social justice and, as such, are both "equally" well intentioned. Christopher James of the W. Haywood Burns Institute distinguishes between the treatment of individuals on an interpersonal and on an institutional basis and thereby finds an important role in equality:

> I'm not saying that equality is not our ultimate goal. I am saying that to start treating, say, the Black community "the same as everyone else" at this point in history will not go far enough in terms of achieving true equality. In racial justice, equality should be the interpersonal standard. On an individual basis, we should all treat

each other the same regardless of race. However, on a systemic level – including individuals acting in an official capacity within systems – the standard must be equity.

(MacArthur Foundation, 2021)

In education, the distinction between equality and equity is extremely important. It is not just that equity is better, but that the espousal and practice of equality can be deeply damaging. Education policies that promote equality dominate the educational landscape and are defended on the basis of a "desire for translation, agreement and univocity" (Derrida, 1992, p. 78). However, they create a forgetfulness of certain people, most notably those with special needs, black and minority ethnic students, and individuals from disadvantaged backgrounds. When, through equality, these groups receive the same as everyone else – identical treatment rather than adapted treatment – they are simply left without enough.

The consequences of being left without enough are stark. The COVID-19 pandemic exacerbated the disparities and heightened vulnerabilities among students with special needs, black and ethnic minority students, and indigenous and disadvantaged students (Qureshi, 2020). In considering each of these groups in turn, we will reflect on how they experienced the pandemic. We want to be clear, however, that the inequities for these groups were already deeply embedded in education systems throughout the world. COVID-19 simply made things so much worse.

Students with special needs experience, somewhat paradoxically, both neglect of, and excessive attention to, their needs and to them as learners. On the one hand, neglect comes through the forgetfulness of them that arises within and through those policies which, as we argue above, privilege equality. The excessive attention to their needs emerges within a highly pathologising and deficit-oriented "SEN industry" (Tomlinson, 2012, p. 267), the growth of which has been "irresistible" (Tomlinson, 2012, p. 267). Children with special needs are, thus, both neglected and rendered highly visible. Teachers work under enormous pressure and try to do everything they can to meet the needs of all children in their classrooms. The support that teachers receive, however, from the "big glossies" (Brantlinger, 2006, p. 45), textbooks that reinforce children's pathologies and from resourcing models that require children's deficits to be specified and measured, reinforce a view of diversity as something that is both problematic and to be *managed*. Consequently, teachers have reported feeling confused about what inclusion is supposed to be and do, frustration that they cannot meet all children's needs, guilt at letting children and their families down, and exhaustion (Allan, 2008).

Schools' response to the pandemic, following government guidance, was to prioritise those children deemed "vulnerable", and these were not necessarily always children with special needs (although it usually included those with the most significant needs) but were most importantly those who might be at risk were they to be left to learn at home. The UK government's definition of vulnerable, for example, included those "on the edge of receiving" social work care or support, adopted children, those who were at risk of becoming NEET (not in education or training), children in temporary accommodation, young carers, children experiencing difficulties in engaging with learning at home (for example because of no access to technology devices or the Internet or a lack of study space), care leavers, and those needing support for their mental health (GOV.UK, 2019). School places in the UK were available to the children of key workers, for example those working in the health sector. Not all teachers were able to secure a school place even though they were doing the vital work of teaching other people's children. In other countries, the option was not available since the majority of schools were closed (UNICEF, 2021).

Black and minority ethnic students across the world experience higher exclusion rates, lower attainment rates, and more frequent placement in special schools (Ladson-Billings, 2021). Darling-Hammond (2001) suggests that in the US, black children are more likely to be taught by less effective or inexperienced teachers. Furthermore, according to Ladson-Billings (2021, p. 69) "teacher discretion" operates in socioeconomically disadvantaged areas, affecting student outcomes. That the problem of inequity "resides squarely inside the schools" (Ladson-Billings, 2021, p. 69) is not without question: "These schools suspend, expel, retain, assign to special education, and deny entrance into gifted/talented and [Advanced Placement] courses for Black students" (Ladson-Billings, 2021, p. 69).

Some contrasting approaches to "race" and racism can be seen in the US and the UK. In the US, there is what Annamma, Connor, and Ferri (2016, p. 156) call "color-evasiveness", oriented to a "goal of erasure" (Annamma, Connor, and Ferri, 2016, p. 156). In the UK, on the other hand, there is a kind of "inexplicitness" (Kirp, 1979, p. 289) – or avoidance – of "race" and racism. Inexplicitness denotes a "preference for consensual, incremental decision making, which is threatened by the confrontational, potentially revolutionary, nature of a racial orientation" (Kirp, 1979, p. 289). Each term, and the approach associated with it, is "neither innocent nor passive" (Gillborn, 2019, p. 114), and each translates into school practices which are governed by whiteness, representing "an enemy in plain sight" (Gillborn, 2019, p. 117). The basis of the enmity within education systems lies, as Annamma, Connor, and Ferri (2016) point out, in the legacy of efforts to *prove* the inferiority, in terms of ability, of certain groups on the basis of their "race". These efforts were first documented by Du Bois at the start of the twentieth century (Du Bois, 1920; 1989 [1904]) and remain ingrained in systems of categorisation, labelling, and classification (Artiles and Trent, 1994; Erevelles, 2000; Baglieri and Llavani, 2020). Consequently, in addition to the disadvantages for black and minority ethnic students described above, they are also disproportionately represented in special education (Annamma, Connor, and Ferri, 2016; Harry and Klinger, 2014).

All of these inequities for black and minority ethnic students existed long before the COVID-19 pandemic, but have undoubtedly been made worse. The pandemic has had a disproportionately greater impact on black and ethnic minority populations (Garg, Kim, and Whitaker, 2020; Owen, Carmona, and Pomeroy, 2020; Herenkohl et al., 2021), with high proportions of deaths. This is associated with the social disadvantage of many black and minority families and the effects of low incomes, limited access to health care, and the likelihood that their working environments were poorly protected from COVID-19, especially in the early stages (Owen, Carmona, and Pomeroy, 2020; Yancy, 2020, McGeehan, 2020). The impact of the pandemic was to expose the nation's vulnerabilities – the educational disparities for black and minority ethnic students, but also health care and economic and climate weaknesses (Ladson-Billings, 2021). Amidst the desperate clamouring to a return to normal (Roy, 2020), Ladson-Billings (2021) points out that getting back to normal is the last thing black and minority ethnic students need: "normal is where the problems reside" (Ladson-Billings, 2021, p. 68) and where oppression and failure prevails.

Students from low-income families, many of whom also are from black and minority ethnic groups (Reay, 2020), experience further disadvantage within schools and schooling. Whilst poverty inevitably has a key role in relation to academic success (Wilkinson and Pickett, 2009), more influential is the "paternal and punitive benevolence" (Tomlinson, 2021, p. 61) that exists within schools and which marginalises and excludes working class young people (Richardson and Powell, 2011). Gewirtz, Ball, and Bowe (1995) have highlighted that students from disadvantaged backgrounds may, like black and minority students, be disproportionately placed in low status and under-resourced schools where their potential to achieve success is diminished. Others have suggested that schooling has an important function in maintaining class divisions and advantages for certain groups of students, with practices such as assessment and testing inflicting "injuries of class [that] are particularly raw and vivid" (Reay, 2020, p. 82). As Reay (2020, p. 318) reminds us, "long before stockpiling became endemic under the pandemic, the privileged in society have been stockpiling educational advantage".

The COVID-19 pandemic affected low-income families particularly badly, with difficulties arising from greater exposure of adults to COVID-19 in their workplaces, reduced income and other forms of financial support (including provision for food), and living in cramped conditions without gardens for exercise (Reay, 2020; Loopstra, 2020) in homes that were "often places of high stress and low solace" (Reay, 2020, p. 315). Limited access to technologies, as we discussed above, made home schooling problematic for some families. There were also differences between schools in the support (both digital and non-digital) they provided children with for their home learning, with schools in disadvantaged areas providing far less (Pidd, 2020; Reay, 2020). Schools in disadvantaged areas have also become, notes Reay (2020, p. 312), a "branch of social services", providing for those welfare needs of children where the state has failed to deliver. School closures in disadvantaged areas, thus, had a far greater impact, creating significant deprivation for children and families and causing psychological damage (Blundell et al., 2020). Giannini and Grant Lewis (2020) underlined the devastating impact of the school closures during the COVID-19 pandemic on disadvantaged children:

> Confinement and school closures often have longer-term consequences, especially for the most vulnerable and marginalized, magnifying already-existing disparities within the education system. In addition to the missed opportunities for learning, many children and youth lose access to healthy meals, and are subjected to economic and social stress.

Warning against "short term fixes", Giannini and Grant Lewis also advocate a key role for education in assisting in the recovery from the pandemic and preventing and mitigating the effects of future crises.

A socially just education?

The inequities and injustices that existed before the COVID-19 pandemic became magnified and exacerbated by it, affecting most of all students with special needs, black and minority ethnic students, and disadvantaged students. As we hasten to get our lives back to normal, we should heed Ladson-Billing's (2021) warning that what was normal for many children was inequitable and unjust. We should also be guided by Ladson-Billing (2006) towards a recognition of the debts that we owe our children, not just as a result of the pandemic but through the damage done to them through our education systems and within our schools. Ladson-Billings distinguishes four types of debt that constitute an educational debt: a historical debt, which in American Indian education is "particularly egregious" (Ladson-Billings, 2006, p. 5); an economic debt, arising from the disparities that exist between schools and the resourcing of them; a sociopolitical debt, whereby black and ethnic minority communities are excluded from civil processes; and a moral debt, which is the "disparity between what we know is right and what we actually do". Apprehending the educational debt is far better than worrying about "learning loss" or about the achievement gap, a major concern for governments and policymakers. It will, however, require a great deal of imagination on our part to construct images that represent the scale of the debt:

> The images should remind us that the cumulative effect of poor education, poor housing, poor health care, and poor government services creates a bifurcated society that leaves more than its children behind. The images should compel us to deploy our knowledge, skills, and

> expertise to alleviate the suffering of the least of these. They are the images that compelled our attention during Hurricane Katrina. Here, for the first time in a very long time, the nation – indeed the world – was confronted with the magnitude of poverty that exists in America.
>
> (Ladson-Billings, 2006, p. 10)

Ladson-Billings points out that such an apprehension of debt and its scale is more likely to guide us towards equity and justice and to forge a "better educational future" (Ladson-Billings, 2006, p. 9). This book is an attempt to contribute to that better educational future with understanding, through the lives of professionals in several countries. Through their stories, we uncover the how, why, and where of inequities within the grammar of schooling. We also follow their lines of flight out of the grammar of schooling and try to rewrite this in ways that are inclusive, equitable, and socially just.

In the next chapter, we discuss the "grammar of schooling" and how it divides students according to racialised and ableist categories, preferring certain forms of knowledge to others along geographical and modernist lines, splintering knowledge into subjects and fracturing learning. Examples are provided from teachers in the DIGITAL project, whereby they either recognise and are critical of the grammar of schooling or contribute to its repetition. These examples help to uncover why the grammar of schooling is so persistent.

2
The repetition of the grammar of schooling

In 1986, Larry Cuban, an historian of education, published a book that sought to disentangle the "perennial paradox facing public schools [in the United States]: constancy amidst change" (Cuban, 1986, p. 1). Beginning the book with a picture of a teacher in an airplane cabin with a chalkboard next to her, while teaching seven children sitting at school desks, Cuban wanted to draw attention to the persistence of certain patterns, rules, materials, and artefacts in education that, even if removed from their usual context, would constantly resemble a traditional classroom.

Tyack and Tobin (1994, p. 454) describe this consistency as part of "a grammar of schooling", referring to "the regular structures and rules that organise the work of instruction" that has remained mostly unchanged and stable over time and decades and that operationalises, according to Zhao (2020, p. 29), "schools' purpose of education". Whilst some changes or intentions to change did occur, in particular during the 1960s and 1970s when the de-schooling movement became (internationally) vocal (Illich, 1972/2006; Holt, 1972/2017), schools and schooling have resisted change, and relations of power within classrooms continue to shape the management of individuals, families, and groups according to certain defined organisational rules.

Wondering why the grammar of schooling has not changed substantially through time and why attempts to challenge it did not succeed, Hunter (1996, p. 147) argues for a "shift in the axis of analysis [from] the subordination of educational principles to a concern with what might be called the *habitus* of the school itself" (italics in the original). To do so, Tyack and Tobin (1994, p. 455) suggest moving the focus from what happens in classrooms to "the organisational framework that shapes the conditions under which teachers instruct students". Ball (2013) maintains that this organisational framework and the grammar of schools are mobilised, and indeed delimited, by relations of power and knowledge systematised within an *epistemic grid*. This epistemic grid provides a perspective on the world and ourselves, shaping an "understanding of the world which is specific to a time and place" (Kendall and Wickham, 1999, p. 67; see also Foucault, 1972). It is a grid that not only orders things (Foucault, 2008) but also makes educational subjects and aims of schooling intelligible, according to certain truths connected to historical and contextual necessities and contingencies.

The grammar of schooling is a historical product which finds its epistemic inception in the late eighteenth and nineteenth centuries in the Global North, and particularly in Europe, with its roots in the Enlightenment period. The Enlightenment, as the cradle of modernity, positioned scientific knowledge as the only possible guidance whereby truth can be found in reality. It ordered things, people, and systems of knowledge on a global scale, imposing the scientific Eurocentric thought with its modalities of thinking, doing, and being (Santos, 2018). By doing so, it made impossible and untrue all systems of knowledge that could provide different experiences of learning and being in the world, in particular those of the Global South (Mignolo, 2011).

A brief history of the grammar of schooling and the modern Western school

The modern school was invented in the Western part of the world, mobilised by this epistemic grid and hierarchies of power that were taking shape between the Global North and South in the second half of the nineteenth century. Answering to a need for governing growing populations according to certain national values, morality, and productivity, the school as an institution emerged at the intersection of newly born nation-states and a fast-growing capitalist reason fuelled by imperialist ambitions. The grammar of schooling is therefore connected and mobilised according to certain forms of control, management, equity, and productivity of the student population, and its formation as desired citizenry along Eurocentric and Global North lines (Armstrong, Armstrong, and Spandagou, 2010). It made the school as an institution one of "the major sites of our social intelligibility … for who we are and what we might become" (Ball and Collet-Sabé, 2021, p. 4).

Fostered by the belief that education could develop children's minds and skills to their full potential, cultivate a cooperating citizenry, and better train workforce in an increasingly economised state, mainstream schooling as we know it was thought to be the solution to the problems of the modern capitalist society. The teacher as the authority, the figure of morality embodying the state, emerged within these premises. Pedagogy, curriculum, and assessment became "a set of practices, arrangements, and techniques aimed at governing individuals in a continuous, regular, and permanent fashion" (Ball and Collet-Sabé, 2021, p. 2). The school as an institution materialised as "a purpose-built pedagogical environment assembled from a mix of physical and moral elements: special architectures; devices for organising space and time; body techniques; practices of surveillance and supervision; pedagogical relationships; procedures of administration and examination" (Hunter, 1996, p. 147). Ball (2013, p. 46) provides a vivid description of its workings, which we report here at length:

> We could take the classroom as a paradigm of discipline in these senses. It is fundamentally organized in these terms. Learners are 'seen' and 'modified' and 'broken down', by age and sometimes by gender, by ability, by 'need', in relation to talents and other forms of specialty or abnormality. Schools are broken down into houses, the school day into a timetable and a curriculum (a serial space of serial knowledges) and into specialist locations; pupil movements are broken down within and into lessons, they are allocated to seats, organized onto tables or in rows, labelled, tested, measured and calculated by the techniques of examination. Literacy and writing, grading and examination, were developed as forms of discipline and differentiation, locating learners within a grammocentric world in which human abilities could be calculated and compared.

From here, the tenets of the modern school became the intersections between beliefs of redemption and upskilling; scientific effectiveness of programmes to understand and train the child's minds; the cure of the body and the discipline of it, and by extension, the discipline of the family (Rose, 1999). Foucault (2008) identified these practices as biopolitical strategies, in which individual abilities, ages, housing, wealth, and health came to be descriptors of the whole population, aided by statistics as the science of the state (Hacking, 1991), to normalise, regulate, and control the population and its ability to contribute to the national wealth. Discourses of race, ability, and class began to emerge, with learners becoming organised in relation to their actual abilities and potentials, as a "question of power", that is related to "who is included, by whom, in which institutional conditions, by what means, and towards what outcomes" (Nguyen, 2019, p. 29).

This process of managing an increasingly diverse student population always happens in relation to a process of normalisation which sorts, categorises, ranks, and creates flows according to certain criteria, molar lines, and expectations, "an entanglement of physical cultural, cognitive and emotional elements" (Ball and Collet-Sabé, 2021, p. 4). Through dividing practices, as "modes of manipulation that combine the mediation of a science (or pseudo-science) and the practice of exclusion" (Rabinow, 1984, p. 8) the school, and indeed the special school and its special pedagogies, became a site where multiplicity and individuality were governed, making visible, and most often excluding, those children and education subjects that were seen as a threat to the morality and productivity of the state. The "dual foundations of grammar" (Deleuze and Guattari,

1987, p. 76) separated the productive from the unproductive, the moral from the immoral, the rich from the poor, the white from the black, the healthy from the unhealthy, through dividing practices that produced breaks within the school population and among learners themselves.

The state here began to intersect the biological, the material, the disciplinary, and the normal as strategies of societal control. This was perfectly encapsulated by the schoolchildren of the School of Barbiana, describing their educational experiences in public schools before enrolling in the democratic School of Barbiana, founded in the 1960s in Italy and directed by Don Lorenzo Milani, a progressive critical educator.

> In elementary school, the state offered a second-rate school. Five classes in one classroom. One fifth of the school I was entitled to.
> It is the system that they use in America to create the differences between whites and blacks. Worst school for the poor from an early age.
> (School of Barbiana, 1990, p. 10)

Dividing bodies, minds, and spaces within the emerging school, the State works to "render us as normal (or abnormal), as exceptional/gifted or as having 'special needs', as educated/educable, or not" (Ball and Collet-Sabé, 2021, p. 5) and began to materialise the legitimate subject of (state) education as male, white, Western, heterosexual, middle class, and able. The failing counterparts were those who could not comply with normal schooling with its time schedule, subject division, performance demands, and standardised pedagogies. They were the most surveilled, visible, and requiring of intervention or separation from the rest of the group; otherwise, they would delay, interrupt, disrupt the *natural process of the other children's development*. A typographical obsession (Armstrong, 2003) came to characterise and label the experience of those who could not be disciplined, sit properly, keep up with the curriculum, the not healthy (or wealthy) enough (the *backward, imbecile, dull, handicapped, emotionally disturbed, with learning difficulties, with disabilities, with special educational needs, neurodivergent,* or *neurodiverse*). Observed and assessed by experts in the fields of medicine and psychology, children were pathologised and rendered curable or discardable in hospital schools, special schools, separated classrooms, pupil referral units, alternative provisions, ability grouping, and boarding schools for indigenous people; what Danforth, Taff, and Ferguson (2008, p. 4) identified as "convenient laboratories for the great Enlightenment experiment – 'improving' people via education (primarily of the senses) and 'moral treatment'". The system of categorisation and control intersected with the practices of examination, as a combination of the "techniques of an observing hierarchy and those of a normalising judgement" and a means to enact "a perpetual comparison of each and all that made it possible to measure and judge" (Foucault, 1977, p. 197–198). Consequentially, individuality was introduced into the files of documentation, with psychological tests of intelligence and practices of observation becoming techniques to frame, fix, and file difference and deviance. Indeed, as Rose (1999, p. 139) points out, not only did the intelligence test produce the identity of "the feeble-minded child" but such identity was also adopted by "eugenicists [who] saw the feeble-minded as a central element in the degeneracy or deterioration of the race".

The grammar of schooling established a certain standard, *the normal child of the regular school,* the child that could be nurtured, cultivated, morally trained, and made into a pliant and respectable citizen. It relied on notions of economic betterment, indicators of learning and teaching outcomes, and "data to measure progress toward institutional performance targets and improvement goals" (Williamson, 2021, p. 19), as techniques, technologies, and strategies continued to classify children, ranking them according to their potential, their bodies, and their minds, in particular through:

i) Pedagogical techniques (categorisation and division, observation, time schedules, surveillance, exclusion);

ii) A set of experts and their knowledge (medicine and psycho-sciences) and figures of authorities – apparatuses (teachers and para-educators);

iii) Certain spaces where interventions took place (schools, classrooms, special schools, and boarding schools); and

iv) Culturally specific (Western) values (productivity and its connection with the economy, order, and disciplined behaviour).

Despite these endurances, during the pandemic, discourses about digital innovation, disruption of the grammar of schooling, and potential for more inclusive school systems seemed to have gained traction. However, technologies entered the already existing breaks, discrimination, and systems of exclusions of the modern school, contributing to new forms of educational and social vulnerability.

From physical to digital: The repetition of the grammar of schooling during the COVID-19 pandemic

Since the emergence of mainstream schooling, technologies have always been understood and mobilised as means of communicating knowledge and as pedagogical strategies to enhance teaching in the classroom (Cranmer, 2021). With education becoming compulsory, and classes more numerous, "many educators have dreamed of making instruction both productive and enriching; wishing that children somehow could learn more and faster while teachers taught less" (Cuban, 1986, p. 3). This dream has persisted, Cuban (1986, p. 4) argues, every time that a new technological invention could "revolutionise the classroom", from the radio to the television and computers. Addressing it as the "unrelenting cycle" of technology innovation, Cuban (1986, p. 4) cites technologies as crucial elements of the grammar of schooling, arguing how, throughout history, each new technology was welcomed with a wave of promotional enthusiasm, anticipating progress in teacher practice and student learning, and promising "individualised instruction, relief of the tedium of repetitive activities, and presentation of content beyond what was available to a classroom teacher".

The "unrelenting cycle" repeated itself during the COVID-19 pandemic, when the widespread use of digital technology to access remote learning was presented as an opportunity to rethink education and schooling for the coming digital era along more inclusive and equitable lines. Promoters of technologies welcomed the global experiment that the pandemic made possible (Williamson, 2021), with technologies positioned as the only viable solution to keep education and learning going (Selwyn et al., 2020). The apparent disruption of the grammar of schooling seemed gigantic: the disappearance of the physical classroom, the pause on examinations, the interruption of school routines, the challenge of reduced visibility and teachers' physical authority, and the rapid switch to digital learning and teaching all pointed to an epistemic shift (Zhao, 2020). The digital revolution had finally arrived, and it was set to rethink, ameliorate, and make more effective the processes of inclusive education through digital technologies (Giannini, 2020).

Yet technologies again entered old cracks, stable hierarchies, and crystallised power relations (Selwyn, 2013). The systems of thought and Eurocentric scientific knowledge, bio-political strategies of normalisation, geographical and spatial orders, and dividing practices constitutive of the grammar of schooling resisted and reproduced themselves in the digital divide (Peruzzo and Allan, 2022). These materialised new forms of exclusions along the old same racialised and ableist lines; digital solutions created new subjectivities and new digital vulnerabilities, where the OECD defined "vulnerable" to:

> [Q]ualify students in a situation of vulnerability and with diverse needs, with an emphasis on … the inclusion of students from an immigrant background; students from ethnic groups, national minorities and Indigenous people; students with special education needs (SEN); gender; gender identity and sexual orientation; and gifted students …. The understanding of the terms

> 'vulnerable students' and the groups they encompass vary across contexts … to emphasize and address the systemic barriers that increase the risk of vulnerability for students.
>
> (OECD, 2020, p. 2)

Vulnerabilities were defined not only by lack of access to digital devices and absence of participation and engagement, but also as threats to the economic prospects of the state. Williamson, Macgilchrist, and Potter (2021, pp. 123–124) point out that research predicted that "skills deficits caused by school and campus closures result in weaker workforce capacity", therefore jeopardising the economic development of countries by eventually producing a "reduced income for individuals and overall 'human capital' deficiencies for nations".

Looking into the persistence and shifts in the grammar of schooling enables us to challenge "simplistic expectations that educators can revolutionise instruction or increase learners' engagement by a more creative or innovative use of technologies" (Macgilchrist, 2021, p. 244). The creation of new forms of vulnerabilities through an apparent series of changes in the grammar of schooling through technologies was the focus of the series of interviews and discussions we had with educators across the globe for the project DIGITAL in a time of Coronavirus.

During the pandemic, we interviewed educators, teachers, headteachers, teaching assistants, and leaders of grassroots organisations to capture their experiences of the pandemic. Their experiences highlighted the perennial paradox of constancy and change in education (Cuban, 1986), making visible how the production and reiteration of difference, classroom organisation, and hierarchical relations of power persisted during the series of lockdowns, while engendering new forms of vulnerabilities and exclusions in the digital classroom. For example, a geography teacher from a primary school in England explains how their school, alongside many others, transferred their face-to-face activities to the online classroom, keeping their ways of learning and pedagogies the same in the virtual classroom.

> I was working in a school, and actually within a system – so this mirrors a lot of the other schools kind of within that same framework – which very early on in the pandemic just took what they were doing and then transferred that model to an online platform, so that they were using the same structures in terms of the timings of the day, length of lessons, everything was the same, they just moved online and then expected students to kind of sit in front of a computer for the length of the day, and for that then to mediate their learning.

The attempt to move face-to-face education online, with the same organisational structures, timings, and lessons, not only demonstrated the resilience of the grammar of schooling but also of the power structures and the systems of oppression that are enacted through schooling. As we mentioned in the previous chapter, children considered already "vulnerable" prior to the pandemic were put at double risk, creating a "double jeopardy" (UNICEF, 2020b) for those already disadvantaged. Children from black and minority ethnic backgrounds, according to the Social Metrics Commission (2020), became the most adversely affected by online education due to low incomes and slow and unreliable Internet connection, and many of them had only their phone screen to access online learning. The social class attainment gap widened for children in public schools compared to private schools (Cullimane and Montacute, 2020), with children from high-income families benefitting from better access to technologies and more time for home-learning (Harmey and Moss, 2021). Black and other minority children were more likely to find themselves in a crowded house and with little space to meaningfully engage with remote and online learning (Reay, 2020). The crowdedness of their house repeated the crowdedness of those classes that the children of the School of Barbiana reported earlier in the chapter, with children identified with special educational needs and disability or from black and other minority backgrounds more likely to populate those spaces. Moreover, the structure of the grammar and the epistemic grid repeated itself on a global level, with countries in the Global South or in rural areas more likely to find themselves at a digital disadvantage (OECD, 2020).

While governments across the globe, in concert with private businesses and the third sector, assisted low-income and rural families and children and those identified with special educational needs and disability by providing computers, specialist equipment, and educational toys, these services were slow and often unsuccessful (Williamson, Macgilchrist, and Potter, 2021). A number of studies ended up demonstrating how digital technologies, rather than equalising the inequities that the pandemic, instead helped make apparent entrenched existing inequities, favouring certain social groups that were already benefitting from the pre-pandemic status quo

(Macgilchrist, 2021). New forms of (digital) vulnerabilities were being produced, though along the usual old ableist, racist, and classist lines. An Italian educator therefore suggested where the focus of problematisation and critique should rely:

> The problem is that we still live in a situation of epistemic violence; that is, we live in an epistemology, within grids that inevitably lead to these results. Therefore, if one wants to seriously talk about it, we must question the educational paradigm of the West; that is, it is not the Italian school system which is just crap, there are systems that are a little more self-aware, but the episteme in which they are constructed is the same. So in Italy there are ecological niches for the handicapped, in England then maybe there will be separate schools for the handicapped, but in the end the result is the same; that is, we have a system that hides behind divisions and groupings.

By pointing at the epistemic inequities of education systems, starting from the internal divisions of the Italian one, the educator makes visible the problem connected to the epistemic grid that mobilises a grammar of schooling through divisions, categories, according to Western paradigms and systems of thought. The pandemic made them even more apparent but removed the enclosed walls of schools within which *vulnerable* pupils were meant to be included; it also brought societal inequities hidden in special classrooms, rural contexts, crammed houses, and forgotten neighbourhoods to light. Therefore, technologies, while exposing old forms of inequities, also created new individualities, new subjects of (digital) intervention and rehabilitation.

Pandemic and the longed-for return to normality: Contextualising technologies and the enthusiasm for digital inclusion

Juana Sancho-Gil and colleagues (2020) had already predicted how edtech initiatives could fail in the context of the pandemic. They argued that narrow visions of digital technologies as saviours of failing education systems can only become obstacles to improvements and transformation in education. They explored how localised projects do not take into account pedagogical histories, community necessities, and local expertise, set aside how technologies have been utilised in different forms in educational contexts for centuries and have become a "social battlefield" (Feenberg, 1991, p. 14 in Sancho-Gil, Rivera-Vargas, and Miño-Puigcercós, 2020, p. 63). They argued that narrow projects not only distract educators and policy-makers from the challenge of building more inclusive societies, but also leave ample space for action for edtech businesses and their not-so-vested interests in education markets and digital possibilities (Castañeda and Williamson, 2021; Cone et al., 2021).

Moreover, as the emerging critical studies in digital education platforms highlight, the diffusion of digital platforms in education, promoted by edtech businesses and corporations, are creating digital spaces that increasingly "manage pupils' learning", creating "environments focused on the monitoring of their behavior" (Decupeyre, Grimaldi, and Landri, 2021, p. 1) towards successful standardised tests and forms of assessment. The primary teacher of geography indeed expressed his criticality in this sense:

> I didn't want my teaching experience to be mediated in that same way, that's not what I signed up for …. They say that the lessons were all through Teams, Microsoft Teams, the software that we were using, and the expectation was that we then adapted teaching resources to then teach through that sort of platform. But the experience for teacher changes, when you shift online … I think it goes, more fundamentally, to what it is [that] we want out of education and schooling. Because I think a lot of schools shifted to actually reinforce this sense that education and schooling are just for terminal examination and that we're just preparing students for written exams.

Through emerging personalised digital learning techniques relying on artificial intelligence (AI) and machine learning, such management not only ignores the broader social contexts of education, but also relies on algorithms that have been exposed as ableist and racist (Noble, 2018; Hoffman, 2018). Digital data are becoming part of a new biopolitical strategy that reworks the last century's forms of state surveillance to make visible difference through digital forms (Zuboff, 2019), dissipating "the areas of education that rely on various ambiguities and uncertainties" (Selwyn, 2019, p. 12) and shaping curricula and pedagogies on examination and preparation to the test.

Macgilchrist (2021, p. 244) aptly asks "what kinds of sociality and individualities are produced through edtech and associated practice" and how the "enduring *stability* of social, economic and educational inequality" manifests despite technological innovations. The grammar of schooling, during the pandemic, interacted with technologies to reproduce old systems of thoughts and regimes of educational practices, and created new digital visibilities and educationally invisible subjects. Technologies entered, shaped, and re-classified dividing practices according to a new normality, a new natural order of schooling that longed for the "return to normal", to the status quo, but through digital innovation and educational transformation through technologies. Alongside that, new forms of (behavioural) disciplines (Manolev, Sullivan, and Slee, 2019), digital disabilities and disorders, and heterarchical authorities and multi-sector networks (Williamson, Macgilchrist, and Potter, 2021) emerged, mixing public, private, medicine, and psychology (with heavy presence and decisional power of international organisations based in the Global North, i.e. UNESCO, OECD, UNICEF, and the World Bank). It is necessary to analyse and make visible how certain structures, subjectivities, and therefore forms of inequities, invalidation, and exclusion, reiterated themselves during the pandemic through digital technologies. This recognises that "while digital technologies inevitably change, institutional structures such as schools may be slower to shift" (Cranmer, 2021, p. 2).

Digital technologies and the resilience of the grammar of schooling

During the pandemic, the resilience of the grammar of schooling, and the epistemic movements between change and persistence, manifested in the intersection between technologies, dividing practices, educational authorities, and surveillance. They mobilised flows and lines within educational assemblages, objectifying and subjectifying specific social categories of children. Digital vulnerabilities emerged through three material dispositions of things, rules, and practices:

- Micro-exclusions and exclusions between the virtual and the regular classroom;
- Discipline and digital reification of classrooms' material spaces and routinised visibilities; and
- Hierarchical relations of power, authorities, and objectifying techniques of examinations.

Micro-exclusions and exclusions between the virtual and the regular classroom

The grammar of schooling repeated itself by separating those children that pedagogically could not keep up with digital online pedagogies and the curriculum now being taught online. Digital vulnerabilities emerged from the usual dividing practices that separate children identified as having special educational needs from those who do not, following molar lines of withdrawal and individualised learning with support teachers. A support teacher from a primary school in Italy working with a child with Down syndrome shares her experience.

> In May, when the video-lessons began, I asked her [the student] to take part in the first history lesson and the Italian, geography, and science ones too, and that's it, because there was really no kind of connection ... She used her computer and tablet and she clicked on the

> various subjects on the Padlet, and on the different days I attached the tasks that were more or less connected with what the class was doing but in another Padlet …. For Italian history, we limited ourselves to paste the activities that [the child] was doing in their [the whole classroom's] Padlet and the families could look at what she had done.

Through highlighting the concerted practices of micro-exclusions of the less able, the slow, or the different, the support teacher describes a scenario that repeats a grammar of exclusions that dates back in time, reiterating the functional divisions and subjective breaks that the modern school operates on children's bodies, minds, and identities. The child she was supporting during the series of lockdowns found herself excluded on multiple levels. Re-enacting the practices of classroom withdrawal that brings "the 'problem' outside the classroom" (D'Alessio, 2011, p. 75) to teach children identified as disabled or with special educational needs in separated special units, here the support teacher brings the child into the separate digital classroom. Stressing how *"there was really no kind of connection"* with the regular curricula, the support teacher then teaches the child a different, simplified curriculum from the rest of the class, using the same digital platform (Padlet) but separated from the other classmates (her own Padlet alongside the rest of the classroom's Padlet), and different forms of examination tailored to her individual needs. Despite the innovation that the Padlet brought into the classroom – a potentially very inclusive tool both pedagogically and on a curricular level which facilitates sharing and discussion of the whole classroom's work – here the grammar of schooling, a grammar of division along ableist lines, repeats itself, producing disabled and vulnerable subjectivities. The same happened with a support teacher in England, who discusses the inaccessibility of the digital curricula and pedagogy for most of the children she supports, and one in particular:

> I think, for most of the children I work with, everything that was online wasn't accessible …. All the children had one-to-ones because [of] all their different impairments …. There is one child in particular I've been working with over time and she is nonverbal, she is unable to speak English, she's got a series of multiple needs and the way she learns is very sensory. All she does is very sensory, very touchy, listening to things, repetition, lots of repetition doing the same thing …. For her, everything that was online was completely inaccessible …. It is a little bit the same in class; she doesn't access learning, so there's not much of a difference, to be honest.

Differentiated curricula and individualised learning and exclusions from the main classroom happen again through the experience of this support teacher in a primary school in England. The digital turn repeated standardised teaching and learning practices that were already excluding disabled children as forms of classroom management (Slee, 2019), and producing them as digitally vulnerable in need of online one-to-one sessions. Here not only are pupils separated and excluded from the mainstream classrooms through practices of withdrawal, but also individualised through hierarchical relations and separated by curricula that are arboreal and striated, repeating a grammar of schooling that ranks and breaks. This process is made even more explicit by the Italian support teacher, who maintains:

> The risk was to leave her in front of this screen to eat the rubber if no one told her [not to do so] in front of all her classmates, so I preferred to do this, sad choice, but a bit forced to help this little girl. […] I don't know if you understand the situation, but when a colleague is stretched, then certain things are also justifiable, you are very tight, you are in fifth grade, you have to arrange the video-lessons and you are forced [to deliver them] and you did not want to, and there is someone who tells you "give this little girl attention". … In short, it was a bit complicated, she participated very happily in the first three classes, greeted everyone, and then we dedicated ourselves to our totally individualised and differentiated programming.

The support teacher justifies the separation by arguing that her colleagues were burdened by the sudden switch to digital teaching and learning, and how there was no time and space to care for a non-compliant child *eating her rubber*. These "guarantees and assurances (of quality, value added, or enhancement), which are increasingly expected within education, set up an inertia from which it is impossible to break away" (Allan, 2006, p. 126). Practices of withdrawal, differentiation, and simplification of curriculum and pedagogy reproduce digitally the same exclusions. The rhythms of capitalism, the pace of performativity in teaching, and selection of the fittest again exclude and relegate the less able, and make the curriculum less intellectually demanding for "young people who are defined as being unable or unwilling to participate satisfactorily in a system primarily directed towards producing academic and technical elites" (Tomlinson, 1985, p. 157).

Discipline and digital reification of classrooms' material spaces and routinised visibilities

The grammar of schooling was repeated along the very same disciplinary lines of order, routine, and behavioural compliancy needed to govern a diverse student population through standardised practices. The messiness of the first period of lockdowns and the need to quickly adapt to remote teaching and learning raised new problems in terms of management of the classroom, control, and visibility of students. However, these new problems were tackled and "cured" in the same ableist, racist, and pathologising ways. A support teacher in Australia provides an example.

> We've had kids sort of set off for various kinds of assessments; one of my students was diagnosed with ADHD, and it all started falling into place when he started being medicated at the start of lockdown. That was a really great thing for him, because all of a sudden he was present, he was listening, he was doing his work, it was just an incredible turnaround from someone who would just switch off, you know.

The support teacher, called a learning enhancement teacher in the Australian education system, is describing how a student in their school struggled, at the beginning of lockdown, to keep up with online learning. Describing as a relief his diagnosis of Attention Deficit Hyperactivity Disorder, she welcomed the compliancy, pliancy, and discipline that the process of medicalising his condition brought to the individual and to the class as a proxy. Schools are sedentary spaces, organised around enclosed locales and clear hierarchies, which do not admit a child that is "restless, fidgeting in his seat" (Youdell, 2006, p. 126). They are places where "rules bind students to certain flows of activity, deviation from which brings a pathologising regime down upon them" (Allan, 2008, p. 62). Here, medical knowledges and medical expertise entered again these fixities, engendering processes of normalisation of children through techniques of control, "order-words" (Deleuze and Guattari, 1987, p. 75) that command and make visible those who differed from a new digital normality. "Habit", Tyack and Tobin (1994, p. 476) point out, "is a labor-saving device". The grammar of schooling persisted and enabled teachers "to cope with the everyday tasks that school boards, principals, and parents expected them to perform: controlling student behaviour, instructing heterogeneous populations, or sorting people for future roles in school and later life" (Tyack and Tobin, 1994, p. 476). Moreover, as Bourassa (2021, p. 253) argues here, inclusion of all students in the digital classroom becomes a "technology of power", a biopolitical project that largely involves assimilation of disabled students, and the fabrication of pathologised identities to re-establish, indeed command, normality in the digital classroom, rather than a valuing of children's diversity.

The sedentary and disciplinary characterisation of the grammar of schooling also sets the ontological and epistemic limits of being a student of the modern, Western school (Ball and Collet-Sabé, 2021), excluding and leaving adrift whoever does not comply with the requirements of order, discipline, and visibility. An inclusion manager of a school in England provides an example:

> Some families were really hard to reach. I mean, for us, one of the hardest ones … two girls, siblings, travellers, they were really, really hard to reach and hard to engage and we weren't sure if it was because they weren't at home. We discovered over time they were struggling with the technology aspect, but also because they have very high incidence of absence from school and kind of disengaging from school, it was a combination of factors, special educational needs …. Because they were struggling with the online aspect, but then everything coming in, writing was hard, but then, also, they have their own cultural beliefs and traditions and priorities that don't always combine with high levels of school engagement, so that was tricky.

The inclusion manager here is describing how two sisters, belonging to a Roma family, were hard to reach and engage in online teaching and learning during the series of lockdowns in 2020. Intersecting their background, culture, and identification as children with special educational needs, she describes *the combination of factors* that cause them to *struggle with the online aspect*, as well as their low attendance and proficiency. The unquestioned switch to online learning has engendered new subjective vulnerabilities, students and families that fall through the net of institutional support and fall short of possibilities of rehabilitation. New-old multiple processes of intersectional discrimination are then generated. In this case, the two sisters and their family are made invisible because they physically disappear from the school record and radar and their lack of digital skill is problematised as a combination of bio-social-racial factors. An additional layer of problematisation emerges because their culture is at odds with what the school requires and this is translated into low levels of engagement, because they are travellers and often absent. "Schools have a single problem", the schoolchildren of Barbiana (1990, p. 35) put it, "the children they lose", those that "are seen as threats to performance and the raising of standards" (Ball, 2013, p. 109). Roma, gypsy, and traveller pupils are the social categories that are most frequently placed on fixed-term exclusions in the UK, at a rate of 17.42% according to the latest Department for Education's statistics (DfE, 2019). By repeating virtual exclusion practices as tools for classroom management, here schools and screens become the limits of educability and intelligibility: what you cannot see is not educable, exposing the epistemic and ontological limits of the grammar of schooling. Foucault (2004, p. 254) addresses this as "state racism", as "a way of introducing a break into the domain of life that is under power's control: the break between what must live and what must die … it is a way of separating out the groups that exist within a population". It is a "biological type caesura" (Foucault, 2004, p. 255) "a new eugenics" applied to "immutable individual differences" (Gillborn, 2010, p. 232) that digital technologies and online learning enabled by intersecting low expectations, low achievement, and persistent inability to show potential. It is an educational death, an acceptance that some children, due to innate and cultural characteristics, are irremediable, and in times of emergency the health and education of the strongest need to be prioritised for the survival of the country.

Hierarchical relations of power, authorities, and objectifying techniques of examination

The grammar of schooling persisted and remoulded regimes of practices through technologies by reworking the relations between the family, the vulnerable child, and medical professionals. Fluid relations within societies of control (Deleuze, 1990) manifest themselves again in the strategies of power between private and public, medicine and education, and the family and the expert. The inclusion manager from a school in England again provides an example.

> Especially when we did the live sessions, some parents could then see "Oh this is what the rest of the cohort is doing or this is how the other children are attending or behaving during this session, and my child …". Because it was a brief window into the classroom that most of us as parents don't ever have … so they can kind of see a little bit of "Oh, I see this is how the other children participate or this is what their behaviour is like during the session and my child is very different".

Families and parents, during the lockdowns and online teaching and learning, had the chance to see and take part in some of their children's classes and observe them while *at school*. Here the inclusion manager is describing how, by seeing the classroom in its entirety, parents could compare their children's behaviour to others. "To be an individual in the modern sense of the word", Simmons and Masschelein (2015, p. 210) argue, "is to be linked to a totality". Here, new deviant subjectivities emerge from the totality of the classroom and its forms of behavioural management at the intersection of public education, digital realities, and parental responsibilities, merging the private of the house with the public of the digital classroom. As the inclusion manager continues:

> So one of the children that comes to mind was in our year one class, at home with mum. She really developed a much more holistic view of her child and a greater understanding of where his needs were and what supported him well …. This one parent really came to have a good understanding, and she went from being really uncertain about an EP [educational psychologist] referral and observation to being one of the parents that welcomes the EP into a virtual observation and assessment. I was following her son with another device, so that she [the EP] could see how he was behaving in the home and how he interacted with toys, and she asked "what should I put out what would you like to see, you know him, what should I do" and I think it was really through that kind of learning herself through the first period of lockdown where she learned a lot, but then, by the same token, he really thrived. He was largely non-verbal and when he returned to school there was much more spontaneous language, much clearer use of language.

Technologies here enter the grammar of schooling, renewing the "grid of intelligibility within which educational success and failure could be located" (Ball, 2013, p. 91). The inclusion manager describes how this particular mother, after seeing her son behaving differently in the classroom thanks to the possibilities that technologies enabled during the lockdown, resorted to the support of the educational psychologist, who diagnosed her child. While at home, the inclusion manager followed the child with a second camera, so as to observe, capture, and let the mother see his difference. This difference transcended the educational space despite being generated by comparing him to his peers in the classroom; it was innate, as it could be seen also while he was playing with his toys at home. Here, psychology and medicine flow through technologies and strengthen old alliances, creating new techniques of power and enabling new forms of vulnerabilities. First, they enter the family, following the child, to observe him playing. Here, technologies involved the family, and the mother in particular, and sought to provide support to become accustomed to scholastic discipline. A biopolitical project of correction and management productively moves from the classroom to the private sphere, using technologies as means of control, surveillance, and subjective government. It also connects the network of authorities, medical experts, the family, the classroom, and the problematic child through the binary grid of the grammar of schooling and the creation of truths through scientific examination.

A second example from another inclusion manager in England highlights how technologies facilitated and renewed the modalities of specific techniques of surveillance of children that would not conform to the grammar of the classroom.

> I think there was something really valuable about using online live call video conferencing services to be able to do meetings or therapy or consultations, because I found that the parents really engaged well with it when they were offered, and once they understood how it

would work and what the expectation was for them. And I think, you know, we're continuing at the moment to use it for things like: I had an annual review meeting for an EHCP pupil, and being able to have mum who, you know, was going to have to dash off – it was her lunch break but she was at work, she was able to be at the meeting – and the EP was at the meeting and the speech therapist was at the meeting, even though she wasn't on site to see the children that day, and the specialist teacher was in the meeting, even though she's working from home .... And then we were able to, you know, to have the child come and be in the meeting, and then actually on the screen, we had the full team around the child. Otherwise, it tended to be a logistical nightmare trying to organise these things; there was something that kind of allowed me especially with working parents to, kind of, find ways to do this, where they could fit it in.

Describing how the platform that allows for video-conferences enables and facilitates meetings between the team of experts and professionals dealing with children on an Education and Health Care Plan (EHCP), the inclusion manager welcomes technologies in the management of disabled children in the school, adding a new dimension of control and hierarchical decision-making. Here the grammar of schooling, with its dividing and objectifying practices of examination, manifests in the layered intersection of tactics of observation, evaluation, and socio-medical pedagogical assessment. At this intersection, a record of the subject identified as disabled or with special educational needs materialises, so that the medico-psycho-social team, in concert with general and specialised teachers and other education personnel, could pursue a personalised, educational, and didactic programme of therapeutic and rehabilitative interventions. Here, technologies not only reproduce and facilitate old objectifying and normalising practices, but also infuse them with flexibility and reachability, again merging the public and the private. They synchronise the grid of observation and judgement of the disabled child, reaching otherwise inaccessible working mums, and assembling the inclusion manager, the educational psychologist, the speech therapist, and indeed the child, as the object of judgement and assessment. "What is at issue here is the proper exercise of authority, as a productive force in the right disposition of things" (Foucault, 1991, p. 93). The experience of the inclusion manager sheds a light on how medical and special pedagogical knowledges not only depoliticise those practices, but also again enable the nominalist creation of differences as part of those "rituals of power" and "ceremonies of objectification" (Ball, 2013, p. 68) constitutive of "being in" an education system. In this individualising network of control and surveillance, children identified as disabled or with special educational needs continue to be defined in relation to normality (Slee, 2019), with their freedom and space of self-government shaped by medicalising truths and specialised experts. Here, platforms and technologies enable "a regime of visibility in which the observed was distributed within a single common plane of sight" (Rose, 1999, p. 135). The grammar of schooling is so preserved by means of maintaining certain relations of authorities that reiterate, strengthen, and reshape forms of control and surveillance that are integral to the assemblage of the making, and singling out, of children that do not conform to the educational norm.

Emergency strategies, the persistence of the grammar of schooling, and repetitions of exclusion through technologies

> … a lot of schools chose to almost double down and the approaches that they then were employing reinforce those ideas …. Rather than using it [the pandemic] as an opportunity to sort of pause and step away from that in the short term.
>
> (Primary school teacher, England)

Teaching assistant: She [the regular teacher] would set a timetable for the day for literacy, for maths, trying to keep the core learning going. And in the classroom, I taught the same stuff, so I would deliver the same thing that she had on Google Classroom live ….

Francesca: So, it was a sort of repetition in the classroom of what was happening online.

Teaching assistant: Yes, it was exactly the same thing, I would do it live and in person in class and she would do it virtually.

(Teaching assistant, primary school, England)

The inception and persistence of the grammar of schooling expose the lines along which the relationship between constancy and change has endured throughout history. Emerging from the epistemic order, systems of thought and hierarchical relations of power laid down during the Enlightenment period, the modern school as an institution emerged, was shaped, and in turn shaped the grammar starting from the second half of the nineteenth century. Intersecting the inception of capitalism, the affirmation of nation-states, the growing intensity of colonialism, and increasing urbanisation in the Global North, the mainstreaming of schooling was imbued with notions of equalising children's opportunities. The aim to nourish their individual creativity and cultivate cooperation while preparing them to compete became the rationale for teaching and learning practices and the expectation of local authorities and the state (Cuban, 1986). The grammar of schooling since then has organised and provided the rationales, the strategies, the pace, the knowledges, the spaces, the experts, and the truths to govern increasing and diversified populations of students, observing, dividing, judging, and excluding the single child if necessary for the management of the whole classroom.

In the modern school, practices of inclusion, selection, and testing have always coexisted with exclusions, marginalisation, and withdrawals within schools (Armstrong, 2003). In fact, as Slee (2019, p. 914) argues "paradoxically, the infrastructure of inclusive education is applied to monitor, calibrate and segment school populations". Within this system, dividing practices, mobilised by a Westernised system of thought and its scientific knowledge, relentlessly enacted processes of normalisation to single out and make visible those children who disrupt the natural order of schooling, along race, ethnicity, indigeneity, and ability markers and according to economic, moral, and disciplinary objectives. While language changes throughout history, those subjects that are perceived as a threat to the state order and productivity, indeed to the citizenry as a whole, continue to be excluded, marginalised, objectified, and hyper-surveilled as second-class citizens who, as Slee (2013) puts it, are politically predisposed to be excluded. "The school", the schoolchildren of Barbiana (1990, p. 20) said, "is a hospital that treats the healthy and rejects the sick. It is becoming an increasingly irremediable tool of differentiation". Indeed, this differentiation is part of the repetition, under a different guise, of eugenics practices that schools, as the educational arm of the state, enact to sift through the population and its lineage (Gillborn, 2010; Ball, 2013), according to Eurocentric and Westernised systems of knowledge, values, and modalities of being and doing. These hierarchical relations of power were reproduced, again, during the epistemic crisis that the COVID-19 pandemic engendered in education and schooling globally. By mobilising discourses of innovation and revolution through technologies, the digital turn during the pandemic promised enduring changes in the ways in which pedagogy, curricula, and assessment were delivered. However, the resilience of the grammar of schooling not only reproduced and managed difference in the online classroom through the same relations of power, and along the usual ableist, racialised, and classist social markers, but also produced new forms of marginalisation, objectifying and subjectifying students as digital vulnerabilities.

Yet, crises are also moments that open for epistemic changes and critical assessment of the present. Moments of emergencies, controversies, and crises "are thus where power is revealed, as paths to certain futures are sorted out, while other possible futures are closed down" (Williamson, Macgilchrist, and Potter, 2021, p. 118). However, as Tyack and Tobin (1994, p. 455) remark, when innovations took place, they usually took place on the peripheries of the education system, for example industrial education, continuation schools, or special education for pupils "who did not fit the regular candidates for batch processing". The COVID-19 pandemic allowed instead for experimentation in the regular classroom and to begin to rewrite the grammar through technologies, opening lines for new modalities of learning, smoothing the spaces in the school, allowing for processes of deterritorialisation, and connecting communities in convivial, ethical, and non-competitive ways. This is the focus of the next chapter.

3 Rewriting the grammar of schooling

The one hundred languages of children

The child is made of one hundred.

The child has

a hundred languages

a hundred hands

a hundred thoughts

a hundred ways of thinking

of playing, of speaking.

A hundred always

a hundred ways of listening

of marvelling of loving

a hundred joys

for singing and understanding

a hundred worlds

to discover

a hundred worlds

to invent

a hundred worlds

to dream.

The child has

a hundred languages

(and a hundred hundred more)

but they steal ninety-nine.

The schools and the culture

separate the head from the body.

They tell the child:

to think without hands

to do without head

to listen and not to speak

to understand without joy

to love and to marvel

only at Easter and Christmas.

They tell the child:

to discover the world already there

and of the hundred

they steal ninety-nine.

They tell the child:

that work and play

reality and fantasy

science and imagination

sky and earth

reason and dream

are things

that do not belong together.

And thus they tell the child

that the hundred is not there.

The child says:

No way. The hundred is there.

(Malaguzzi, 1996)

The remarkable persistence of the grammar of schooling relates wholly to its unremarkable existence. It is accepted, note Tyack and Tobin (1994, p. 454), as "just the way schools are", and as they also observe, it is only the departure from, or challenge to, customary schooling practice that attracts attention. And as Malaguzzi (1996) vividly demonstrates above, the school's knowledge is assumed to have far greater importance than any of the languages brought by the child, and this dictates what is learned in school. In this chapter, we recount the lived experiences of teachers and school leaders who sought to rewrite the grammar of schooling through their practices. These rewritings were developed during the pandemic, when learning was relocated to the home, when blended learning was introduced, or when the students returned to school. They included finding new, creative ways for the children to learn, smoothing the school and curriculum space and connecting people and places in new ways, for example through new relationships with parents/carers. They also involved using both digital and non-digital technologies in convivial ways. We explore these rewritings, making particular use of Deleuze and Guattari's concepts of smooth and striated spaces, deterritorialisation, the rhizome, and lines of flight, to make sense of them and to consider their inclusivity. Before discussing the teachers' and school leaders' creativity, we offer a brief history of reformists' ambitions for rewriting the grammar of schooling. We begin with John Dewey's progressivism and move to comprehensive education before ending with some contemporary reform efforts and calls to arms by education activists. Each of these three strands of reform has in common a strong and steadfast orientation to equity, and in each case, we focus on what these reforms were a reaction to and how they were enacted.

A brief history of reform

The history of attempts to disrupt the grammar of schooling, according to Larry Cuban (2020, p. 665), is "a dismal tale of disappointment and failure", with, he suggests, bars of steel seeming to hold that grammar in place. Yet, it is not for want of genuine and purposeful effort to reform; nor does it reflect a lack of ambition on the part of the educationists who sought to lead the change.

Dewey and the whole child

The American John Dewey's progressive philosophy, that children learn by doing and that a good education is one that reaches the whole child, emerged in the early part of the twentieth century as a reaction to the discourse of efficiency that had swept through the business sector and was adopted by school administrators and school leaders (Cuban in Heller, 2020). Condemning the inequities in society and fearing a loss of moral and spiritual direction within American society, Dewey advocated a form of active citizenship and common social purpose within schools that children should learn through practice. Schools, thus, were important environments which should not be divorced from social life, but should provide the space where social life can be improved (Dewey, 1899; Apple and Teitelbaum, 2001). Dewey describes what he calls the "moral trinity of the school" (Dewey, 2014, p. 75) as transcending the grammar of schooling:

> The demand is for social intelligence, social power, and social interests. Our resources are (1) the life of the school as a social institution in itself; (2) methods of learning and of doing work; and (3) the school studies or curriculum … in so far as the curriculum is so selected and organized as to provide the material for affording the child a consciousness of the world in which he has to play a part, and the relations he has to meet; in so far as these ends are met, the school is organized on an ethical basis.
>
> (Dewey, 2014, pp. 75–76)

Dewey articulated the key function for education as the co-ordination of the individual child and social factors, making his work, as Biesta (2006) notes, communication-centred rather than child-centred, as it is often misrepresented (Biesta, 2014). Dewey formulated the notion of transaction (developed from his earlier notion of interactions) to denote the activity that goes on in school in between the individual and the social. These transactions take place in nature and interact with it. Pedagogy, in a transactional sense, is the act of co-ordinating the child and the curriculum, and central to this is the child's experience in its entirety: "things – anything, everything, in the ordinary or non-technical use of the term 'thing' – are what they are experienced as" (Dewey, 1905, p. 158). For Dewey, the relationship between experience and knowledge was that knowledge was obtained through the occurrence of experience, and this was a significant shift from traditional forms of knowledge of the world "as it is" to discovering the conditions and consequences of experience (Biesta, 2014).

The colonisation by scientific knowledge of alternative understandings, including "common sense" was a particular concern of Dewey (1939). He was troubled by how this had come to have a hegemonic influence over what was held to be both true and rational. His project, thus, could be described as one of interruption of that hegemony in order to create new understandings of knowledge (Biesta, 2014; Biesta and Burbules, 2003). This necessitates a shift from the domain of certainty to "the domain of the possible" (Biesta, 2014, p. 46), but also requires an orientation to connectivity – between children and the social, between knowledge and experience, and between curriculum and pedagogy.

In spite of the compelling nature of Dewey's ideas for educational reform, some critics have argued that they are incomplete (Noddings, 1998; 2010; Held, 2005), while others have noted their failure to materialise into classroom practice (Apple and Teitelbaum, 2001; Bernstein, 2010). There is little doubt, however, that Dewey's ideas inspired a wave of educational reform and renewal that was international in scale (Biesta and Miedema, 2000; Bruno-Jofré and Schriewer, 2012). Of particular note is Dewey's influence in China, although this rose and fell in accordance with the changing political context in the country.

The comprehensive ideal

The fundamental idea behind the comprehensive school, a school that does not select on the basis of achievement or aptitude, was a rejection of determinism on the basis of class, ethnicity, or ability (Martin, 2015) and, according to Caroline Benn (1982, p. 84), "a comprehensive system is the only way we can openly ensure attention to all equally and at the same time protect and reveal the full range of human gifts". Clyde Chitty, considered the UK's "patron saint of comprehensive education" (Benn and Martin, 2018, p. 11), saw comprehensive schools as interrupting the grammar of schooling with a model of teaching that was acting for and with pupils rather than upon them (Benn and Martin, 2018). This ensured the prevention of the "so-called 'ceiling' of a child's possible achievement" (Chitty, 1979, p. 162). The comprehensive school, thus, was a reaction to the rampant elitism within education that encouraged grammar schools and the selection and teaching of children by ability, which was seen by the comprehensive reformists as a kind of evil:

> It is very important that our comprehensive schools shall not content themselves with merely achieving equal opportunity for the competitive success of individual pupils. In the years ahead, now that the folly of eleven-plus segregation is everywhere being recognized, they will be tempted of the devil. They will be shown

and offered all the scholastic kingdoms, including Oxford and Cambridge, York and Canterbury. Tempting though such prizes are, they must not be tempted to divert the new schools from their larger purpose: the forging of a communal culture by the pursuit of quality with equality, by the education of their pupils in and for democracy, and by the creation of happy, vigorous, local communities in which the school is the focus of social and educational life.

(Pedley, 1970, pp. 205–206)

The conviction that schooling should match children's abilities, a perverse notion of equality of opportunity (Tyack and Cuban, 1995) whereby progress in education meant "a place for every child and every child in its place" (Tyack and Cuban, 1995, p. 20), was fiercely opposed. This was objectional because of the labelling and categorisation that ensued and the fact that educational success was only available to select pupils.

The first comprehensive schools were introduced in the UK in the 1940s, on an experimental basis, before becoming more widely established in the 1960s. Comprehensive schools in the US, often described as public schools, emerged slightly later, in the 1970s, but had begun to gain momentum following the 1954 Supreme Court's decision in Brown v Board of Education. This landmark decision catalysed social action among protest groups to challenge not just racial segregation in education but that of other disadvantaged groups, such as disabled students, immigrants, those from low-income families, and girls (Tyack and Cuban, 1995). Comprehensive schools were promoted actively by the government, who were influenced by the research of

James B. Conant, former President of Harvard University and Ambassador to Germany. Conant urged the widespread adoption of comprehensive schools, with programmes that "correspond to the needs of *all* the youth in the community" (Ravitch, 2001, p. 63), and this in turn provoked a flurry of curriculum reform. In spite of what seemed like an unusually well co-ordinated effort across governments and agencies and an enthusiastic reception in schools, the reforms stalled, overtaken by what Ravitch (2001, p. 49) describes as a "racial revolution". Heightened demands from civil rights groups for integration, equality, and justice in schools following significant racial violence and increased awareness of poverty and deprivation meant that the comprehensive progressivism had to take a back seat: "in the context of such transcending demands, the pedagogical revolution was no revolution at all" (Ravitch, 2001, p. 49).

There has been much criticism of comprehensive and public schools, and even some regrets expressed by the reformists themselves. Concerns in the US about children's functional and cultural literacy, albeit based only on attention to test scores, led a policy commission author and other critics to bemoan the "crisis in schools" (Ravitch, 2001, p. 45) and to declare the US *A Nation at Risk* (National Commission on Excellence in Education, 1983). Criticism has been levelled at schools' lack of comprehensiveness, either because of their failure to include *all* children or because of their largely Eurocentric orientation (Arnot, 1983; Kozol, 1991). Clyde Chitty wishes, on hindsight, that he had placed greater controls over admissions because it was wrong to think comprehensive schools could end divisions in society (Benn and Martin, 2018). There has, however, been much defence of comprehensive and public schools, and at least a branding of the criticism for society's woes as irresponsible (Cremin, 1991; Tyack and Cuban, 1995). Berliner, for example, argues that the public school system of the US has actually done remarkably well as it receives, instructs, and nurtures children who are poor, without health care, and from families and neighbourhoods that are considered dysfunctional (Berliner, cited in Tyack and Cuban, 1995), while Tyack and Cuban (1995, p. 37) themselves suggest that "for all their defects" schools might still be the best thing in some children's lives. Indeed Berliner and Biddle (2001, p. 411) go on to suggest that the so called "crisis in schools" in the US has been manufactured and amounts to "myths, half-truths and sometimes downright lies", with the so-called evidence obtained by misleading methods and misinformation.

Contemporary challenges to the grammar of schooling

There have been calls, since the 1990s to the present, for a radical rethinking of education. Some of these calls have come from governments; for example President Bush enjoined: "For the sake of the future – of our children and the nation – we must transform America's schools" (Tyack and Cuban, 1995, p. 110). The New American Schools Development Corporation (NASDC), charged with advising the Bush administration, issued the challenge that incremental change would not suffice: "assume that the schools we have inherited do not exist" (Tyack and Cuban, 1995, p. 110). This start-again attitude, according to Tyack and Cuban, is a big mistake and has led to the flickering and fading of the "utopian impulses to reinvent schooling" (Tyack and Cuban, 1995, p.

132). The best kind of reform, according to Tyack and Cuban, is one which builds on what is already healthy, and they cite a classroom teacher who captures its experimental nature: "We fell through the day ... like Alice in Wonderland, soaking up ideas, experimenting with and stretching our talents" (Mathews-Burwell, 1994, p. 15).

Similarly in the UK, successive governments have threatened radical overall of the education system, from New Labour's election pledge in 1997 to make "Education, education and education" its three priorities (Fielding, 2001, p. 1) through to the Conservative party's zealous insertion of competition, markets, and choice into education. They achieved this by passing legislation that made provision for new – "free" – schools to be established by parents, communities, or businesses. They have also regularly sought to re-establish grammar schools, arguing that increasing access to these is part of a "fair" system of education that will ultimately increase social mobility (Ball, 2021). Conservative leader David Cameron declared, in a speech in 2011, that there were no alternatives to looking to a reformed education system to ensure society was saved:

> We want to create an education system based on real excellence, with a complete intolerance of failure. Yes, we're ambitious. But today, we've got to be. We've got to be ambitious if we want to compete in the world. When China is going through an educational renaissance, when India is churning our science graduates ... any complacency now would be fatal for our prosperity. And we've got to be ambitious too if we want to mend our broken society. Because education doesn't just give

people the tools to make a good living – it gives them the character to live a good life, to be good citizens.

(Cameron, cited in Ball, 2021, pp. 7–8)

Although the Conservatives claimed that businessification of education would drive up educational standards, it would also, inevitably, be profitable for the businesses themselves. Ball (2007) argues that privatisation in education is much more than reform: it is social transformation that has extreme consequences, altering the meaning of education, teaching, and learning, and "changing the framework of possibilities in which we act" (Ball, 2007, p. 187). The free schools, notes Wilby (2010), have little prospect of addressing inequities in education, since they, like most school types recently invented, will tend to favour the middle classes, who have the time and know-how to take advantage of diversity (Wilby, 2010b).

Recent efforts, in the US, to "upend the grammar of schooling" (Cuban, 2020, p. 669) have resulted in some small victories and bigger defeats. The emergence of hybrids, with some innovation alongside more traditional forms of schooling, along with, in some cases, the creation of new grammars of schooling, has ensured a lack of permanence of progressive reform overall. Cuban (2012) lays the blame at administrators who have wrongly assumed that structural changes will alter traditional teaching approaches and which instead have "left a trail of broken dreams, wrecked careers and 'oops!' from policymakers who have departed for different jobs" (Cuban, 2012, p. 119). Cuban (2008) also highlights how reforms often focus on the wrong thing, citing administrators' fervour for tackling the problem of time (usually by proposing to lengthen the school day) rather than concentrating on improving the quality of the time spent in school. Ball (2021), on the other hand, warns that the political rhetoric around reform often leads to an exaggeration of impact and that real impact in schools is actually very complex and very difficult to achieve (see also Ball, Macguire, and Braun, 2012).

Reviewing educational reform and its discontents, Dahlberg, Moss, and Pence (2007) cite the Italian historian Ginzberg's contention that we are constantly offered solutions before we have considered the correct and critical questions, while White (2007) suggests that we remain locked into nineteenth century values and practices as we try to enter the twenty first century. We also, argue Fielding and Moss (2011), appear to remain convinced that the one magic solution to inequity is around the corner and Zigler's reminder of the need to address the fundamental causes of inequity is salutary:

> Are we sure there is no magic potion that will push poor children into the ranks of the middle class? Only if the potion contains health care, childcare, good housing, sufficient income for every family, child rearing environments free of drugs and violence, support for parents in all their roles, and equal education for all students in school. Without these necessities, only magic will make that happen.
>
> (Zigler, 2003, p. 12)

Thompson (2020, p. 1) is more scathing about the misdirection of reforms, pointing to "explicit corruption and other 'bad behaviour' in the school system". This and the lurid newspaper headlines that they have generated, she argues, have seriously damaged the reputation of (especially English) education and eroded public trust.

The leading academic voices calling for reform propose a range of solutions, but most of them are at the radical end of the spectrum. Pat Thompson (2020, p. xviii) demands a "re-moralisation of government" and a "new contract with the public", while Ladson-Billings (2021, p. 68) calls for a "hard re-set" in education, just as would be done to a malfunctioning digital device, when all other efforts to fix it have failed. This re-setting, most needed in relation to class and race, according to Ladson-Billings (2021), can be achieved by some deep digging into culture and into the lives that students bring to the classroom (Hill, 2009; Emdin, and Adjapong, 2018). Fielding and Moss (2010) spell out what is radical about their proposed reform, taking inspiration from the utopian thinking of Levitas (2008), Wright (2010), and Unger (2004), and involving fundamental rethinking:

> Serious utopianism is a kind of speculative sociology, in that it is both systemic and institutionally specific. It embeds both a philosophical and anthropological quest for the substance of human flourishing, and a sociological quest for its conditions. It is a process of the imaginary reconstitution of society, which involves looking holistically at alternative modes of livelihood and social organisation, exposing them to public debate – as utopian proposals have always done – and considering means of transition.
>
> (Levitas, 2008, p. 90)

For Fielding and Moss, this requires recognition of the profoundly ethical and political nature of education, a point endorsed by

Ball and Collet-Sabé. By declaring schools "intolerable" (Ball and Collet-Sabé, 2021, p. 1), the authors imply that they should not continue to exist in their present form and function. Ball and Collet-Sabé (2021) endorse Clarke's (2020, p. 164) proposition that we should become much more aware of the "distortions and obscenities of power" (Clarke, 2020, p. 164) and the fantasies that they generate, and invite us to "refuse the past once and for all, rather than reform it" (Ball and Collet-Sabé, 2021, p. 12). The alternative education advocated by Ball and Collet-Sabé (2021) is an inclusive one that nevertheless supplants inclusion with relationality and diversity as its key attributes (Olssen, 2003).

Technologies are recognised as having strong potential for reforming education and altering how children learn (Macgilchrist, Allert, and Bruch, 2020; Murphy et al., 2020). However, as we have already noted, there is some ambivalence about the nature of that potential and some concerns about inequities which may actually surface through the use of technologies. There is also some suspicion about the potential misuse of technologies, or rather about the directing of these towards raising the profits of private companies. We return to Illich's (2009) notion of conviviality in respect of technologies and the intention to provide freedom through an interdependence with, rather than enslavement to, technologies.

Among the contemporary voices calling for educational reform, there is a heightened sense of urgency for this to be undertaken as we emerge from the pandemic. Sensing that we have a moment and an opportunity like never before, Reay (2020, p. 320) sees hopeful possibilities in the "growing righteous indignation" at the class and race inequalities that were exacerbated during the pandemic. This, she argues, could incite action towards more inclusive education systems but would be dependent on the establishment of a "collective righteous indignation" (Reay, 2020, p. 320). The need for an education re-set specified by Ladson-Billings (2021) was provoked by the endless calls for a return to normality, and she quotes Roy (2020) to highlight the possibilities that exist in the post-pandemic moment:

> Our minds are still racing back and forth, longing for a return to 'normality', trying to stitch our future to our past and refusing to acknowledge the rupture. But the rupture exists. And in the midst of this terrible despair, it offers us a chance to rethink the doomsday machine we have built for ourselves.
>
> (Roy, 2020, p. 10)

Such a re-set is clearly demanding for teachers and school leaders, as it challenges them to "interrogate their own worldviews and develop the facility to move from the center to the margins" (Ladson-Billings, 2021, p. 77). In so doing, they will come to recognise their own thinking and cultural practices as normative, but this is a necessary shift for the grammar of schooling to be rewritten.

The lived experiences of professionals that we present in the remainder of this chapter do not, individually, represent the kind of utopic visions of the kind outlined by Fielding and Moss (2010), nor are they likely, in themselves, to lead to educational reform. They are, however, radical and represent breaks in and interruptions to the professionals' usual practices and, as such, give glimmers of possibilities for rewriting the grammar of schooling in ways that could lead to wider, larger scale change, and for this to happen in the school. We turn now to these lived experiences.

Insider rewritings

We present a series of "rewritings", consisting of actions by the professionals that were altered ways of doing things which impacted on the identities of students and the professionals themselves and on their lived experiences of education and of schooling. With the assistance of key concepts from Deleuze and Guattari, we uncovered three main types of rewriting, the first of which was *finding new learning lines,* whereby professionals discovered new and creative ways for students to learn, sometimes in response to the children's desires. A second kind of rewriting is what we have termed *smoothing the school,* and involved what Deleuze and Guattari (1987) describe as deterritorialisation, literally smoothing out or disentangling the rigid hierarchies within the school. It also involved a decolonisation of the curriculum that opened up to new knowledges. Finally, we found much rewriting in relation to *connecting people and places,* with professionals strengthening their ties with communities and growing trust with both the communities and the students. We discuss these below.

Finding new learning lines

Teachers, school leaders, and other stakeholders described the significant pressures on them to support the students' learning, whether this was online, at home, or in school for those able to attend. But in responding to these pressures, they also found new and better ways to do things that produced better learning experiences for the students and, in some cases, enabled them to do the kind of teaching that they had always desired, but had been prevented from prior to the pandemic because of the strictures of the grammar of schooling. One principal of a primary school in the US described how the pandemic had provided a moment where creativity was not just possible but necessary:

> The adrenaline of those first few months of, like, creativity and possibility and, like, everything's broken so just do it, you know …. [It] was incredibly thrilling.

This principal identified a moment over the first few months of the pandemic *when chaos and creativity was at its highest*. Another principal of a primary school in Malaysia agreed that the pandemic had brought with it new ways of working and teachers discovered that, when they let go of some of their control, children could learn in new and surprising ways:

> So what the teachers were enjoying … was seeing all their work unfold, so we try as much as we can to move and step back and let the children's learning happen by themselves …. Teachers always want to be in control of the classroom, it's just a natural thing, they feel like if you let go too much you'll just go crazy and out of control …. Sometimes the children start on one topic, and then the conversation goes elsewhere.

Deleuze and Guattari (1987) describe this kind of learning as rhizomic and as very different from the knowledge dispensed within the grammar of schooling "which articulates and hierarchises tracings" (Deleuze and Guattari, 1987, p. 12). Rhizomic learning, in contrast, emphasises experimentation and experience and allows new knowledge to be discovered:

> Expression must break forms, encourage ruptures and new sproutings. When a form is broken, one must reconstruct the content that will necessarily be part of a rupture in the order of things.
>
> (Deleuze and Guattari, 1987, p. 28)

Enjoyment and fun were key elements of learning for the teachers in one school, according to the principal of a primary school in Malaysia:

> Teachers feel that they can take their students anywhere, as long as everybody's safe, and, you know, they can turn the lessons as fun as they like, we always push on fun learning, especially for primary; we want them to feel that they're learning in an enjoyable way.

Also central to finding new lines for learning was following the children's desires. Desire is not something that features ordinarily within schools and could be said to be constrained by the grammar of schooling. Staff spoke, however, of their discovery of students' interests and desires and of their pleasure in being able to ignite and follow these. Desire, for Deleuze and Guattari (1987, p. 399), is always relational and "assembled" rather than pure or natural. This also means that it sets itself going and cannot necessarily be controlled (Olssen, 2009).

One school generated what they called a "passion project" to enable students to follow their desires. Another teacher allowed children to follow their own desires and to choose the materials they preferred to work with, and this was especially important for some students with special needs. In a school in the US, a more structured programme of following children's lines and desires was introduced. Inspired by Carla Shalaby's (2017) *Troublemakers*, the programme, led by a teacher educator who had been working with teachers on a graduate programme, began by teaching anti-oppressive education, disability studies, and critical race theory to students before handing over the teaching to the students themselves. Allowing students to experience their desires produces not just good learning but changes students' minds and bodies through what Deleuze (2004, p. 164) calls "affects". These signal new becomings for both the student and the teacher.

A principal in Malaysia described how she actively encouraged teachers to follow these new creative lines of learning even if they felt uncomfortable with these:

> And every time we cut and say 'okay, let's go back here' you're blocking that creativity that they're going to … they're thinking of other things …. It's still relevant to learning, it's just not what was planned by the teacher, but they're still learning something, right?

The "something" that the students were learning takes place, according to Deleuze and Guattari (1987), not in safe spaces where the learners can be passive but in places where they must participate actively: "A rhizome, a burrow, yes – but not an ivory tower. A line of escape, yes – but not a refuge" (Deleuze and Guattari, 1987, p. 41).

A school principal described the invention of a new subject, called "do it yourself", for the students to experience at home: What began as a half day on DIY during lockdown was a response to a perception that children were becoming tired out by online learning. The DIY activity importantly involved no screen time and was so successful it was extended to an entire day.

New lines of learning were found in a balance between digital and non-digital technologies, including nature in the latter. One arts teacher in a primary school in Chile allowed children to find their own new lines of learning through art:

> I gave them the possibility to choose their own topic, I was teaching them just the basic ideas about an art installation. And then I was telling them you could use whatever you want …. We talked about the importance of how art speaks, it is a language … some of the art pieces are really personal.

This teacher used an approach inspired by Reggio Emilia to engage the children's senses and to literally create new lines of learning:

> So I was looking for something that you have to touch, so also something that you have to listen, also that you have to move [yourself] …. I remember the theremin, you have to move your hand and then you could draw lines with your hand and then you have the sound because of this movement [she moves her arm and hand again]. And I was telling them that this is like a magical instrument, you know, because you don't have to touch it, but you have, you can listen to the music … and then they were drawing lines in the air and then

you could listen to music, so then they were, like, more than the hand and also we were looking at concert theremin concert and they were like oh imitating the sound. Then they have to use … a piece of wood, and then they have to follow the sound with the wood with paint, so they were doing, like, straight lines and curved lines, and they were like making this, like, massive painting following the music and imagining it was a straight line or a curve line, and they were like doing this. And that was online, you know …. In their own houses.

The teachers' discoveries of new lines for children to learn along appeared successfully to interrupt the grammar of schooling by opening up new possibilities, new experiences, and new becomings. Sometimes these new lines came from the students themselves and their desires; the courage of the teachers allowed them to flow. The new lines of learning produced *affect* for the students and potentially altered their subjectivities, with the far reaching significance of "affective pedagogy" underlined by Grossberg (1997, p. 387):

> [An] affective pedagogy [is a] pedagogy of possibilities …. It is a pedagogy that aims not to predefine its outcome (even in terms of some imagined value of emancipation or democracy) but to empower its students to begin to reconstruct their world in new ways, and to rearticulate their future.

The challenge to the grammar of schooling afforded by these new lines of learning and the affect they created do not constitute seismic ruptures, but rather productive and creative interruptions which allow the students to deviate playfully and to return to more familiar ground when needed or desired.

Smoothing the school

Partly in order to ease some of the pressures on the students, as well as on themselves, and partly because of the opportunities afforded by the pandemic, the professionals sought and found ways of working differently from how they had previously – "normally" – practised. These new practices had the effect of smoothing the school and the space occupied by the curriculum and opening up to new knowledge and new learning. Deleuze and Guattari (1987) define these smoothing practices as deterritorialisation, and they appear to have the potential to unpick the grammar of schooling by working on its rigid lines and hierarchies. As we argued in Chapter 1, schools hierarchise and regulate the movement of students – literally – as well as the relationships (among the students and with teachers) and the acquisition of knowledge. Deterritorialisation works on breaking this down and undoing "processes of continuous control and instantaneous communication" (Smith, 1998, p. 264). Mindful of those practices of surveillance and management that we discussed in Chapter 2, deterritorialisation here is both a breaking of existing codes and a "making" (Howard, 1998, p. 115) that provides an escape and yet opens up to new intensities.

A teaching assistant in a primary school in England described the school space as becoming smoother by virtue of comprising smaller groups, and as benefiting some children particularly because of its reduced intensity and pressure and because of *who was actually more on board, more present, and their learning progressed.* It was also more conducive to learning for all students:

> I think it will make learning more accessible, you know, for everybody, and I think children being always busy, and always kind of engaged, in that sense, it's not always productive, so if we think about productivity, I think, if … the aim of society is productivity this is not conducive to productivity; I mean being super busy, and super back to back, etc., it is not necessarily productive.

Some teachers smoothed the school space by slowing down and taking more breaks; this in turn alerted them to how crammed and intense students' lives had been when things were "normal". In order to smooth the space of school while it was online at home and help children and their families manage work at home, one school introduced a system for differentiating activities as *must do, should do, and could do*, with the *must dos* covering the core activities of English, maths, and science to ensure that these were completed.

Teachers also found ways to smooth the space occupied by the curriculum and this opened up a space for new knowledges and new learning. One teacher in a primary school in Chile, for example, found a means of bringing past and present together to enable children to engage with indigenous culture which had previously been presented to them as part of the non-living world:

> The other day we were talking about objects and I was telling them that the activity was to try to think about an object that speaks about the past and the present. So we were seeing this and that is indeed indigenous that comes from an indigenous culture. That they are they used to neat baskets you know …. In the general history, they say that all of them are dead, this culture. But it's not true because there are some of them that are still alive and they are trying, and they are making a, like, a big effort to keep it alive, you know, the culture in terms of language and in terms in terms of culture and … way of living …. I found this documentary where you could see these, like, old ladies still knitting these baskets and teaching their families … this idea of knowledge … it's passed on from [one] generation to another …. I was showing this to the students … the idea of thinking about the objects and how the objects are important and how they are, like, history in a way.

This had generated huge excitement among the children, one of whom had particularly impressed the teacher by presenting a protective mask as an object of the present which would become something of the past. Parents also became interested in this project and, as we discuss later, this contributed towards strengthening the community.

Culture and knowledge of the local community became a huge focal point for students in a US school, as a primary school teacher explains:

> There's a local project, the Puerto Rican History project, where they're capturing, we have a really significant Puerto Rican community in [place] …. In the city

archives, there's nothing about them; there's one tax record from the 1950s, there's nothing about the Puerto Rican parade and, I mean, the bilingual schools that they started here. We had one of the largest air drops after hurricane Maria to Puerto Rico … there's none of that in the curriculum, so we did that. We talked about some of the really powerful movements for racial justice and schools that were done in the city. We spoke about the various disabled activists that were here [in the city] and so that was our curriculum … just focusing on local knowledge.

This project was generated by students who were part of an innovative programme of activism, which we discuss further in the next section.

Another primary school teacher in England sought to access alternatives to the dominant knowledges of the Global North. In translating a climate nature course into other languages, he became aware of the extent of the dominance and this led him to alter his practice. This teacher worked with the young people within a climate action group, Youthtopia (https://youthtopia.world), to modify some of the language and learning, leading to a critical approach:

> So that course is about indigenous knowledge and the idea of actually being quite critical of a lot of the structures within society, and in one of the activities actually exploring the idea of the kind of societal norms, that so much of what we do is simply because it's accepted as the norm and rather than actually saying it's the best way to do this, so it's like one of the

> analogies is the idea of saying that burning fossil fuels is just accepted as a norm rather than questioning it … in terms of a practice.

Another teacher also contended that new knowledges could be found beyond the Global North that offer *completely new ways of thinking* rather than *just confirm the things you already know*. These new knowledges, and the digital and non-digital technologies that had enabled students to access and acquire them, were exciting and beautiful to the professionals and they expressed a desire for these to remain open to the students.

The teachers who worked on smoothing the space of the school and the curriculum achieved a level of decolonialisation which seems likely to undermine the grammar of schooling. They appear to have succeeded through an explicit "turning away" (Hickey-Moodey, 2009, p. 178) from the Global North knowledges, which is also in itself a becoming, and by actively seeking out the unheard voices. Exposing students to these new voices is likely to further contribute to *affect* for the students and to their altered subjectivities. Those instances where students were involved in political projects, for example of translation, are likely to have drawn students' attention to the intersecting of different axes of oppression – economic, political, cultural, psychic, subjective, and experiential – that produce disadvantage and oppression for some (Brah and Phoenix, 2004). At the very least, they will have become more aware of the intersubjectivity of their own selves and of the identities of others as diasporic (Brah, 1996), with students and teachers alike occupying a space where:

> multiple subject positions are juxtaposed, contested, proclaimed, or disavowed; where the permitted and

> the prohibited perpetually interrogate; and where the accepted and the transgressive imperceptibly mingle.
>
> (Brah, 1996, p. 208)

This newly smoothed space, in the school and the curriculum, is thus an exciting one that is full of new possibilities and new ways of relating and being together in the world.

Connecting people and places

Teachers, teacher leaders, and other stakeholders succeeded in disrupting the grammar of schooling by rewriting the connection between schools, the people within them, and the communities in which they were located. In one case, this involved moving out from behind the school walls. Invariably, it involved working on the existing power relations and hierarchies and undermining or dismantling them.

A great deal of emphasis was placed on ensuring students and their families felt well supported during the pandemic and strenuous efforts were made in this regard. One principal in a Malaysian school went further to secure "buy in" from parents by according them the status and role as "co-teachers":

> I said we're all doing our best for the children, so we need your help to work hand in hand, so we gave them the name co-teachers, please be our co-teachers from home because we cannot reach the children, and that time lockdown was very strict only two people could go for groceries, and, you know, that's all you could do, so we really needed their help.

This changed community, with parents as co-teachers, took some time to establish but eventually became the norm.

A newly appointed principal described the building of community as their first and most important role. This principal described as *exhilarating* their discovery that they could build a community online, *even in these like square boxes* (Principal, US). For this principal, the online platform created an interdependency between children and adults, including adults at home, which was extremely conducive to good learning and they described one student who had done far better as a consequence than they would have done in the classroom environment.

The grassroots education leader from Italy literally stepped beyond the walls of the school to connect with those students who had already been hard to reach before the pandemic. He distributed what he called *parcels of the mind* which, just like food parcels, contained items, in this case books, notebooks, tablets, and stories, that were actually a pretext for making physical contact with these students. He described the success:

> And we did these three-minute meetings that were called "spaced meetings of the third kind" because we had to … the spaced meetings of the first type are the WhatsApp, the spaced meetings of the second type are the zooms, and the spaced meetings of the third type we are close, no trouble to touch each other, but we see each other and we can also exchange a few words, and this was fundamental and I think that we were able to reach addresses that were not even on Google Maps because there are places that are unknown, illegal buildings, non-existent roads, that is, roads that exist

> in reality but do not exist in the maps, so it was really an important operation which we say has somehow transformed the virtual community into a physical community and the physical community into a virtual community.

The teacher described connecting with these students as a smart combining of physical and virtual territory. The Chilean teacher's work with history and with objects associated with indigenous cultures, as we have previously mentioned, generated great interest among the parents and, as a result, strengthened community ties. The act of decolonising the curriculum, thus, seems to have assisted in the strengthening the bonds with the community. One teacher was convinced that communities were a better locus for learning than school. This teacher recalled instances, during the pandemic, when groups of parents had organised themselves to deliver home schooling collectively.

A teaching assistant in a primary school in England described how technology had kept an already strong school community connected:

> There is a very strong, you know, kind of closeknit community around the school, and there is a sense that the school is actually a reference point. … a place of trust …. Really the main intent of the school was a very strong sense of inclusivity, solidarity, which are really values that go across. The main idea was to keep contact and keep being that point of contact for the families, so that was, in that sense, Google Classroom.

For the grassroots organisation leader and educator from Italy, technology had enabled new connections between people and places which, in turn, had enabled the recognition of certain debts, for example to the Māori community. For this leader, technology, and the communication fostered by it, could also enable education to be more civic in its orientation, exposing children to the absurdities in the world:

> Certainly, this is the reality of the means of communication, that is, the means of communication and technologies put us constantly in contact with social reality and all the absurdities it contains. You know that one of our slogans is this verse of Danilo Dolci "there are those who teach without hiding the absurdity that is in the world, but dreaming of each one as today is not". So we must not hide the absurdity that is in the world.

Trust was an important element for strengthening connections, and several professionals described their efforts to grow this trust as they supported students and their families during the pandemic. Trust is the extent to which people believe others are acting for the public good (Fukuyama, 2001), as well as an expectation that they will be treated fairly (Uslaner, 2002). Altering the power relations within the school community was an important way of growing trust, and in one school, this was realised on the online platforms by giving the children the role of host. The principal of this school also grew trust by giving the children opportunities to teach something to the rest of the class. Often this was some technological knowledge or skill which the children had mastered, and the principal found that it was easier to hand this over to the children online than in the classroom, as "in the classroom ... that would have been a much more controlled experience".

The Troublemakers project in the US involved handing significant power and control over to the students and this, in turn, strengthened trust and achieved equity:

> It's all about just disrupting the flow of power in schools ... so when we really listen to students, we can transform, we can do better. They are the experts of their own lives, so it's all about trying to engage in a practice around that.

The importance of trust was underlined by a teacher from England who spoke of what it meant to his students and their families:

> They've got a really finely tuned bullshit detector, they trusted us. The families trust us. And you can't fake that.

Uslaner (2002, p. 1) echoes this teacher's appreciation of trust, describing it as a kind of "chicken soup of social life". In other words, trust delivers good things and makes you feel better, but, like chicken soup, it works in mysterious ways.

The strengthened connections with communities and the networks that ensue are means of affirming desire, according to Deleuze and Guattari (1987). This in turn leads to a maintenance and circulation of both desire and the connections: "to connect is to affirm, and to affirm, to connect" (Rajchman, 2000, p. 13). Bringing desire to the fore in the relations is an act of language for Deleuze (2004) that literally makes language stutter and cracks open words and things. The naming of parents as co-teachers is a good example of such a profound language act.

Teachers and leaders had to make explicit efforts to connect with communities in ways that they had not managed prior to the pandemic. Perhaps the desire for connection may have come from necessity; the need to have parents "on side" for the learning that took place at home. It seemed, however, to cultivate a greater respect for parents and communities and what they could bring to education, and this is a significant departure from the deficit-orientations towards parents and lack of trust that have been inscribed within the grammar of schooling.

Changing places, spaces, and subjectivities

In spite of efforts over the years to reform education, and amid the voluble calls for change, the grammar of schooling has persisted, and the many languages that Malaguzzi (1996) suggests children bring continue to be ignored. Yet, whilst, as we reported in Chapter 2, many of the professionals we spoke to contributed to the maintenance of that grammar, we also found many instances of it being challenged. The crisis that was the pandemic also opened up a space for doing things differently, not least by exposing the constraining nature of the grammar of schooling. Consequently, teachers, teacher leaders, and other stakeholders discovered new lines of learning for their students to follow, found that they could reduce or remove some of the rigid hierarchies and boundaries within the school space and effectively make it smoother, and actively enhanced the connections between people and places. These are substantial challenges which also amount to new becomings and altered subjectivities for the students and their families, as well as for their families and communities. From these becomings "ever new, differently distributed 'heres' and 'nows'" emerge (Deleuze, 2004, p. xix). The danger is that these openings and becomings are lost as things return to "normal" and as the grammar of schooling becomes reinstated. The challenge for us, therefore, is to identify the possibilities for the sustainability of these insider rewritings. We take up this challenge in the final chapter whereby we consider the possibilities of avoiding a return to a certain normal, or creating a "new normal", and for rewriting the grammar of schooling with a grammar of becoming.

4
Unsettling identities for a socially just inclusion?

And if we keep doing what their grandparents had as an education offer … then we'll keep getting the same results, because it's universally true if you keep doing the same thing you'll keep getting the same results. So, why, if we know that, would we do that? We need to do something different, we need a paradigm shift.

(Teacher, England)

We must have an open didactics … and we must have open knowledge …. Internet and technologies are indispensable because they allow us to range in all areas, in all directions, and again if we return to that definition of technology, it is not the device but the set of relationships that are established around a technological object, but also to the thought that is established … around this technological object …. We need an idea that abolishes the encyclopedia to move on to what I called before, navigation skills, go from a closed or lockable knowledge to an open knowledge.

(Educator and grassroots organisation leader, Italy)

> What really saved us as a team, as a school, is the creativity of the teachers, because I always push on creativity, I said, "you know your children, you know what they would love to do", so they pushed, they really thought out of the box and they are already used to that because [that] culture is already in our school.
>
> (Principal, Malaysia)

In this final chapter, we offer our reflections on the lived experiences of the teachers and school leaders and how the specific educational spaces of the school and, during the pandemic, the home have been encountered and *lived*. We also consider how these experiences appear to have shaped the identities of students. In keeping with the focus on lived experiences, and in the hope of encouraging others to undertake work of this kind, we begin, in dialogue, with some reflections about our own lived experiences of doing this research and of writing this book. We then offer some thoughts on the possibilities for the sustainability of the new inventive and creative practices that teachers told us about.

Julie: It will be great to reflect on the lived experiences of the professionals that we've heard about, but first off, might we take a moment to consider our own lived experiences of doing this research and writing this book?

Francesca: While interviewing teachers and professionals during the series of lockdowns, I was amazed by how they were all trying to reinvent themselves and to challenge and escape certain predispositions and dispositions of educational objectives and schooling during the pandemic. Going through the transcripts of such powerful conversations, I realised how enduring, entrenched, and recursive certain practices of exclusion were in the modern forms of schooling. However, this moment of crisis, in which major disruptions happened to education systems around the world, showed the old cracks and the blossoms of new possibilities, a new grammar of multiplicities, that technologies enabled in their digital and non-digital forms. The idea of the book emerged as a form of engagement with the old, new, and recursive forms of educational exclusions and inclusions. The aim was to show how the old persists and takes new configurations according to the contextual and historical contingencies, and how the new always finds a space to emerge, making visible ways of doing and being in education. This reminds us how there are always more inclusive and considerate alternatives than the ones that comfortably adapt to an exclusionary and profit-based norm. The book is an invitation to make manifest how different ways of doing education are already there and that there are teachers, professionals, pupils, who are already enacting them. The writing of this book gave us hope, and I hope it will do the same to whoever thinks it is worthwhile to read, and act upon it.

Julie: I feel immensely fortunate to have had the opportunity to carry out this research and to have had the financial support of the YTL Foundation, Malaysia. It was even more gratifying to have been encouraged by a major philanthropist who heads this organisation to ask the big questions about the pandemic and the educational responses to it. As we asked these questions, even bigger questions began to surface about education, or rather schooling, and the inequities it produces. And again, we were strongly encouraged to ask these big, fundamental questions – so we did. The pandemic, terrible as it was, nevertheless enabled us to both look at its effects and shine a light on the inequities that were already there in the education system.

It has been great to publish the findings in academic journals and books (Peruzzo and Allan, 2022) and to present papers at conferences, but when an email notification about the *Lived Places* series came through, I felt very excited. This series seemed to offer us a unique opportunity to ensure that the lived experiences of the teachers, teacher leaders, and other stakeholders could be brought to life and shown in all their colour and texture. It has been marvellous to try to do this and to ensure that we do justice to their lived experiences, but it has also been challenging as we have had to leave a lot of wonderful material out.

I want to come back to the experiences of working with some of the theoretical ideas. But first, what about the lived experiences of the teachers you interviewed? Were there any surprises for you?

Francesca: What came as the biggest surprise to me were the spaces, the pockets of creativity that such an ominous moment created in order to think education and schooling differently. The teachers I listened to readjusted and reinvented their teaching and pedagogical practices in a way that could reach, meaningfully, all children. Yet they did not do that in prescriptive and prescribed ways. In such a terrible moment, those teachers would still make children and families feel cared for, as well as followed and empowered in the use of technologies, whether digital or analogue. Children, teachers, and principals embraced the present moment and explored modalities of being educators and being in education that fostered connections, relied on community knowledge, built on love for teaching and pupils. They made of the moment a learning experience that can shift the ways in which we do education. We want the examples and accounts we used in the book to create surprise for our readers too. Borrowing Santos' words (2018, p. 59), these teachers, leaders, principals, and support teachers are "intermediaries between collective knowledge and the group or community as a whole", individuals that dare, through their practices, to enable multiplicities in education and different ways of being in education, upholding socially just practices and forms of thought that connect the Global North and South in meaningful, and decolonised, modalities.

Julie: I too was surprised (and rather delighted) by the creativity among teachers and leaders and I will come to this later. But my first – and greatest – surprise perhaps should not have been a surprise at all, given what we already know. It was the sheer strength and persistence of the grammar of schooling and the ease with which it was replicated even under the extreme circumstances of the pandemic. We recognised, as we discussed in Chapter 2, that the establishment of the grammar of schooling has a long history and roots in the Global North of the eighteenth century. And as we note in Chapter 3, there have been some very ambitious attempts at reform and at undoing the grammar of schooling, all of which have failed. The Global Partnership for Education (2020) signalled that the pandemic presented an opportunity to rethink education and find new mechanisms to support and enhance accessibility. It is perhaps naive to have thought this was possible. Professionals were, of course, working to try to make everything as normal as possible for children and their families during the pandemic as they were forced to do all their learning from home. But as Ladson-Billings (2021) has reminded us, the so-called "normal" is far from ideal for many children and can often lead to inequities. And so we heard from the teachers about many instances of the grammar of schooling being repeated and sometimes even reinforced.

Francesca: What surprised me in this regard was how easily the reproduction of exclusions materialised through technologies. The chaos of the early months of the pandemic first accelerated the spread of beliefs that digital technologies were the only solutions to the disruptions that the pandemic had brought to education systems around the world. Second, very quickly they rematerialised old exclusions, producing pupils and families as digital vulnerabilities when they could not be reached through, or keep up with, digital teaching and learning strategies. However, these new vulnerabilities entered old cracks, those "breaks" that we referred to in Chapter 2, and while being treated as "new problems", they repeated the same grammar of exclusions and marginalisations, in particular along the lines of ability, race, gender, class, and geography.

It was surprising how quickly those divisions on bodies, minds, and subjectivities became reiterated in the virtual classroom, with disabled students taught in break-out rooms or in different virtual meetings altogether, with differentiated curricula and pedagogies. In Chapter 2, we showed how many of them became the exclusive responsibility of the specialised teachers, while regular teachers attempted to keep up with a digital turn, virtual classes to manage, and new material to be produced. Perhaps it is not a surprise that modalities of teaching and learning had been repeated online. The rapidity that was required of schools and teachers to adapt to this new modality of delivering content left little room to stop and think about how inclusion could be best done through technologies, in ways that included all children without having to rely on a rather clumsy and uneven distribution of technological devices.

It was rather surprising to hear how technologies could become devices that exclude families and pupils that could not use or access them, but also how they could become instruments of extreme visibility. On the one hand, we were struck by the experience of the two Roma siblings who just disappeared from the school radar because they were difficult to manage through the system of inclusion put in place by the school. On the other hand, we noted how new disabilities were made visible through digital technologies. We think the example of the boy who was diagnosed with ADHD because of his inability to sit in front of a screen for prolonged hours was emblematic. The rapidity with which a certain norm repeated itself in controlling pupils that could not adapt to the new (digital) schooling urged us to analyse and problematise the new intersections between technologies, medicine, and the persistency of the grammar of schooling. We were also dismayed by the surveillance of *vulnerable* children that technologies enabled.

Additional cameras extended the control of children's behaviour at home and further medicalisation of difference outside the classroom, and this left us very concerned about the power of technologies in producing new divisions and medicalised differences. Indeed, the experiences that we could access and hear through the accounts of teachers, teaching assistants, principals, parents, and grassroots organisations' leaders during the pandemic elicited surprises and concerns, especially when technologies were clearly instruments that contributed to the production of new inequities, exclusion, and vulnerabilities. However, they also left us with surprises that were more hopeful.

Julie: They most certainly did surprise us in more optimistic ways and the inventiveness and creativity of teachers and leaders during the pandemic was truly awe-inspiring. The new practices that emerged included finding new lines of learning and creative ways for the children to learn; smoothing the school and curriculum spaces and some of the hierarchies within these; and connecting people and places in new ways, for example through new relationships with parents or carers. Many of these were developed as ways of coping with the difficult circumstances of overseeing children's learning at home and the subsequent return to school, and the teachers and principals were pleasantly surprised at what often turned out to be better ways of working and better ways of learning for the children. The new learning lines that teachers found often involved the outdoors, or were discovered in response to particular desires of the children which the teachers followed. It almost always involved fun. The spaces of the school and the curriculum, which we have documented as key elements in the grammar of schooling, could, the teachers found, be smoothed out and some of the hierarchies, which had previously appeared fixed, could be softened. And, finally, teachers discovered new and more respectful ways of connecting with parents and carers, as well as students, especially when reaching out to them in their homes. The ultimate surprise for us was the extent to which these new practices could potentially alter the subjectivities of the children and their families. This seemed possible through the children learning new things or learning in new ways (and therefore surprising themselves); by being exposed to new knowledges, for example about indigenous cultures, and by enjoying, together with their families, better relationships with school and the professionals within it.

The excitement of recognising the potential of teachers' new practices to alter the children's subjectivities was tempered by the risk of not retaining these practices – through reterritorialisation.

Before thinking about how we try to retain these practices, I wonder if we might reflect on how useful the theoretical ideas that we used were in understanding and making sense of the potential impact of the teachers' lived experiences?

Francesca: Epistemology, more than theory itself, shapes our understanding, thinking, seeing, and being in the world, and as Ball (2010, p. 67) reminds us, it is "a starting point for thinking differently about the social world, thinking between existing positions, and thinking against mindless orthodoxies". The idea of working through and with theory to make visible the alternatives to the "fully-digital" solutions provided during the pandemic can really help thinking about different and more equitable education presents and futures. In particular, the notion of the epistemic grid that we borrowed from Foucault (2005) provided us with a theoretical tool to see how limited solutions to crisis and emergence moments, such as the COVID-19 pandemic, are dictated by a certain order of power relations. It is the power of the status quo, the comfort of the norm, and, more simplistically, the conveniency of the "what is already there". The idea of an epistemic grid is also useful to capture the *hows* of the grammar of schooling and its repetition of exclusion along the usual lines of race, ability, gender, indigeneity, and class, and the *whys* it has perdured for such a long time, despite numerous efforts to change it.

The epistemic grid is also helpful to problematise and question the dynamics and rationale that shape our routines and mundane practices of schooling. Underpinned by a scientific and objective approach to truth and sustained by scientific knowledges such as economics, biology, linguistics, medicine and psy-sciences, the epistemic grid continues to mobilise the grammar of schooling through hierarchical relations in favour of professionals and through a fast, capitalistic pace of education. However, it also relentlessly relies on divisive practices that mark, label, discriminate and ultimately exclude children that do not fit within a certain (normalised) idea of citizenry shaped according to Global North criteria.

Conversely, the epistemic grid is not only a useful device to explore the practices and effects of the grammar of schooling *within schools*. Santos (2018, p. 3) talks about an "abyssal line" which elicits ways of knowing that concern the practices, knowledges, and experiences in the Global South that have been invalidated by the advent of modernity in the Global North. This abyssal line, which defines the limits of the epistemic grid, produces absences and invalidates plurality of experiences through making them non-existent in educational communities and beyond. With the research project first, and with the book later, we sought to problematise the grammar of schooling as *within* the epistemic grid, and attempted to find instances, during the pandemic, that cross that abyssal line, showing how the process of decolonising education and schooling is indivisible from expanding the possibilities of being and doing differently and more equitably in education. And indeed, technologies, in their digital and non-digital form, contributed substantially to such process.

Julie: The most helpful ideas for me were those of the philosophers Deleuze and Guattari (1987) and in particular the rhizome and deterritorialisation. They really helped in discovering the potential of the teachers' new practices for altering the children's subjectivities. We heard from the teachers about discovering new ways for the children to learn which seemed to be free from the usual constraints and which went off in new and surprising directions. Deleuze and Guattari's idea of the rhizome seemed to capture this perfectly, since, as rhizomes in real life, such as the strawberry plant, they grow in unpredictable ways: underground and unseen. The suggestion from Deleuze and Guattari that these new learnings also create new becomings, new ways of being a child and a learner, seemed very apt and rather exciting.

I also found Deleuze and Guattari's notion of deterritorialisation particularly helpful in understanding what the teachers were telling us about trying to work in ways that were simpler, smoother – and better. Deterritorialisation, a word that Deleuze and Guattari invented, depicts a smoothing of the space and removal of some of the rigid lines and hierarchies – and this seemed to capture perfectly what the teachers were doing. This became even more apparent when teachers worked on the curriculum space to smooth it out and to seek out knowledges that had not previously been accessible to them or to the students. Recognising the teachers' work as deterritorialisation helped, in turn, to see its power and potential to interrupt the grammar of schooling.

Deterritorialisation was also invaluable in alerting us to the risk that these new, highly inventive practices of the teachers would not be retained and would be lost through a process of reterritorialisation and through a return to the grammar of schooling. Reterritorialisation is a condition that Deleuze and Guattari recognise well and depict vividly:

> You make a rupture, make a line of flight, yet there is still a danger that you will reencounter organizations that restratify everything, formations that restore power to a signifier, attributions that reconstitute a subject – anything you like, from Oedipal resurgences to fascist concretions.
> (Deleuze and Guattari, 1987, p. 9)

In the final section of this chapter, we consider how the creative and inventive practices of the teachers and the rewritings of the grammar of schooling might be retained.

Sustainable becomings

The kinds of becomings that were possible through the teachers' actions, and the leaders' endorsement and support of these actions will not happen on their own. They require particular commitments to be made and for these to be accompanied by an openness to new possibilities. We outline the commitments which are suggested by the research, indicate some possibilities that these commitments might provoke, and pose question for school leaders and teachers.

Learning to live with – and love – uncertainty

This commitment underlines the importance of being open to creativity on the part of teachers and surprises in what the children do and learn. It offers possibilities for trying new ways of teaching and for children's discoveries to bring pleasure rather than fear. As Hannah Arendt points out, this is an act of love which has the potential to save children from ruin, "where we decide whether we love our children enough … not to strike from their hands the chance of undertaking something new, something unforeseen by us" (Arendt, 2006, p. 196). Schools and educational communities are often criticised because they "do not keep up" with changes in wider society, and this discourse was reiterated during the pandemic, when teachers and leaders were accused of being too far "behind" the digital transformation that was needed. This commitment encourages leaders to ask themselves:

- How can I actively encourage teachers to try new things in the classroom?
- How might I validate and celebrate outcomes that are different from those in the formal curriculum?
- How can processes of digitalisation and digital technologies support innovation in a way that does not stifle teachers' creativity?
- How can learning management systems enhance and strengthen the relations between the school community in a way that is not superimposed?

Teachers might pose the following questions to themselves:

- What new things can I bring into the classroom?
- How will I react to surprises that the children bring to the lesson?
- How can digital technologies and learning platforms support and enhance my teaching and learning expertise in creative ways?

These questions invite reflection on how schools and education communities can become spaces for daring and beacons for change in society, embracing uncertainty and contingencies as fruitful components of educational lives and practices.

Trusting teachers to do the "right" thing

The narrative that teachers are reluctant to embrace the "novelty" of (digital) technologies in their teaching practices and therefore hinder schools' progress has been repeating itself for a long time. During the pandemic, this happened again. However, changes and innovation in schools and education communities do not occur just because teachers are told that they will become gatekeepers of new technologies. Indeed, teachers play a crucial part in the process of transformation, but they need positive reinforcement, trust in and recognition of their abilities, and a solid leadership in order to succeed. The "uniformed systemic prescription from above and mistrust" (Lingard, 2014, p. 69) that arises from standardisation with education policy, metrics, and accountability practices provokes Ball (2013) to ask "how not to be governed in that way?" We invite school leaders to pose the same question to themselves, and encourage them to consider whether they might govern differently and support teachers' creativity and "critical thinking as the primary element allowing the possibility for change" (hooks, 1994, p. 202). School leaders might ask questions such as:

- To what extent am I fostering teachers' creativity in the classroom?
- How can I move outside of accountability frameworks and trust teachers to do what they do well?
- Can I embed teachers' expertise, listen proactively to their doubts, and trust them to choose the right technologies to integrate in the processes of teaching and learning?

On the other hand, teachers might ask themselves questions that place their work in a bigger systemic picture:

- What systemic, political, economic, and cultural barriers are hindering me from changing my practice?
- What reflective practices can I use to draw upon my life and work experience to reinvent/rethink my role as a teacher?
- How can children's experiences spur different ways of teaching and learning in my classroom?
- How can I share the good practices I have explored and developed in my teaching and learning as well as voice my fears, doubts, and uncertainties relating to digital technologies?

This commitment supports a vision and rationale of teachers as individuals that are "full" of potential and discourages a deficit-oriented approach to their use and knowledge of technologies that blames them for slow changes in pedagogy and curricula.

Embedding children's experiences and desires in the design of technologies

During the pandemic technologies, including digital platforms and connections through digital devices such as laptops, tables, and mobile phones, became a necessity that was hardly questioned. This was intertwined with new forms of exclusions generated by children's and families' *digital poverty*. To engage children in learning processes, it is necessary to commit to also letting them make their own relationship with technologies. This commitment concerns a flexible strategy in the adoption and use of technologies for pedagogical purposes, in ways that are adaptable and malleable to children's desires and enhancement of their educational experiences. Illich (2009) called such an approach to technologies *convivial* in that technologies should support the accomplishment of a purpose that has been chosen by the user. Such use of technologies is intended to be experience-led, enquiry-based, and fostering of children's self-development by centring their experiences in non-medicalising and fluid ways. This commitment would require school leadership to ask:

- Are the technologies and platforms the school uses free to use in a way that is equitable?
- To what extent are the desires and life experiences of the school community taken into consideration in the choice of adopting certain digital technologies?

Teachers respectively might ask questions on:

- Does children's mastery of technologies enhance their abilities? Are they constrained when they use such technologies in the classroom?

- How can I embed children's life experiences and desires in my use of technology in my classroom?

These questions invite the problematisation of the processes whereby certain technologies are "imposed" on educational communities and indeed children, hindering their opportunities to reinvent themselves through their use and to enhance their learning experiences in ways that are unexpected, adaptable, and equitable.

Ensuring inclusive and context-based practices in all aspects of teaching and learning

The pandemic contributed to the circulation of a discourse of digital inclusion, focusing on teaching and learning practices through technologies as the solution to enhance inclusive education in the classroom. However, this shift prevented reflections on how inequities and exclusions have already been entrenched before the pandemic. Inclusive education is a process, not an end, and it has not yet been successfully enacted in either the Global North or South. In this condition of globality, inclusive education urges questions on "how to live together" (De Lissovoy, 2010, p. 280), with a need to be sensitive to difference in ways that start with differences and do not deny them. It urges educators to celebrate local histories and cultures that might have been hidden or oppressed by global hierarchies, and to support "more sensitive orientation to relationships, both within the classroom and at the level of the imagination of global society" (De Lissovoy, 2010, p. 281). This includes mobilising digital and non-digital technologies through pedagogies that draw upon local expertise and involve families and communities in an active way, that centre children's experiences in the school and community's aims and histories, and that open doors to new imaginaries and futures. Questions that leaders can ask themselves to uphold such commitments are:

- How is the school supporting and upholding local histories, cultures, and expertise?
- How am I facilitating the development of an inclusive school community?
- How am I engaging teachers from a variety of backgrounds and abilities so that children can identify themselves in relation to them?
- How can digital technologies and devices support and foster the promotion, relations, and connection with local communities, organisations and their expertise and the school and educational community?

Teachers instead could enquire into their practices and ask:

- Do my teaching and learning practices draw upon children's lives and respect cultural and ability differences?
- Is my teaching relevant to, and does it draw upon, community knowledges and expertise?
- Are my pedagogies and curricula recognising global forms of oppressions in terms of ability, gender, social background, indigeneity, race, and ethnicity?
- How can digital technologies and devices support and foster the promotion and integration of local expertise, culture, and histories in the educational community's activities, curriculum, and pedagogies?

These questions invoke pedagogies that dissolve the notion of abilities in loci of possibilities and curiosity. They help to shift towards the enactment of inclusive education by expanding the practical imagination of teachers, children, and leaders towards more globally and locally socially just educational communities.

Enabling flexibility in knowledge, time, and space

The research project and the book explored how a certain grammar of schooling repeated itself during the pandemic. Old marginalisations and new exclusions have materialised beyond the school walls and through digital platforms. Grek and Landri (2021, p. 395) talk about "overlapping regimes of topologies and temporalities", with acceleration being essential to deliver remote teaching and learning practices. However, it is exactly this acceleration that prevented alternative and more critical modalities of rethinking schooling and its grammar during the lockdowns. This final commitment invites school communities to rethink the accelerated, disciplinary, and contained materiality of schooling by centring teachers' and children's times and pace and co-operating towards flexibilisation of spaces, using technologies as appropriate. It also invites a smoothing of hierarchies of knowledges, allowing for interdisciplinarity and cross-fertilisation of scientific and community knowledges. Here, questions that leaders can ask themselves might include:

- How can I structure my school timetable in a way that supports flexibility of learning around children's preferences and desires?

- Does the school timetable facilitate enough interdisciplinarity and cross-fertilisation of scientific and community knowledge?
- How can digital technologies open up the school and connect the educational community to a multiplicity of local and global knowledges and experiences to expand its imaginaries and teaching and learning practices?

Teachers instead might ask themselves:

- How can I introduce flexibility in my practices in terms of timetabling and children's pace of learning?
- How can collaborations with colleagues and the local community diversify my curriculum and favour interdisciplinarity and cross-fertilisation of knowledges?
- How can I use the school and community's space in a way that is more flexible, making the school's walls more porous?

This list is by no means exhaustive, and we invite leaders, teachers, and others to propose further commitments, along with accompanying possibilities and questions that they provoke.

We turn now to some practical suggestions that could open up spaces and opportunities for doing things differently and for enabling new subjectivities and new becomings – for the whole educational community.

Rewriting the grammar of schooling: Where to begin?

Whilst we in no sense intend to re-invoke the hierarchies that are such a problematic aspect of the grammar of schooling, we nevertheless consider that the senior leadership of the school has to be supportive of, and engaged in, any reform and rewriting. Change, we propose, has to come from within the school, but the senior leaders have to be open and receptive to this change. We suggest below a number of practical activities that could be undertaken throughout the school.

A whole school overhaul of the grammar of schooling

An entire overhaul of the grammar of schooling could be initiated by upending the power relations within schools and going directly to the children, teachers, and parents/carers and communities. Centring children's desires and experiences of schooling, technologies, and the pandemic; teachers' ideas on how to reform pedagogies and curricula in ways that make space for digital technologies, while respecting their existing expertise; and families' experiences of remote learning, use of technologies, and priorities in their children's futures; are all vital for this overhaul. Senior leaders might facilitate the centring of the insights from these key individuals – and then stand back.

Student-led reworkings

Students could be engaged in activities whereby they identify problematic aspects of their school lives and learning and help to rework it in better ways. This necessarily involves rethinking existing teaching and learning practices and relationships in the classroom, including: children's experiences, desires, and culturally relevant practices and knowledges in curricula; teachers reshaping their role as also learners and listeners; and dialogical and peer learning that can support activities such as children as teachers and intra-class and inter-generational pedagogical activities and forms of assessment.

Teacher-led projects on curriculum rewriting

Staff with particular expertise, for example on decolonising the curriculum, or who themselves bring diversity to the school, e.g., in ethnicity or disability, could be invited to lead the rewriting of an area of the curriculum. The results of this could be reviewed and any adjustments made before extending it to other curriculum areas. Decolonising the curriculum implies both changing and critically informing education content and problematising pedagogies and ways of learning. Training and hands-on workshops on culturally relevant pedagogies and universal design for learning for teachers, families, and the senior leadership team, with a particular focus on digital technologies, could support the development of socially just change in schooling and educational communities beyond schools' walls.

Experimentation workshops

Schools might host workshops that invite teachers to try something new in their teaching, including different ways of integrating technologies in their teaching and learning activities. Teachers could script these collectively within the workshops, take these away to try out in their classrooms, and then return to share experiences. This experimentation, and the experience and responses of children in different subjects, will be important material for reflection on novelty that can be brought in or adjustments that can be made.

Parents, carers, and communities in partnership and in alliance

The key role parents and carers had as educators during the pandemic, recognised and formalised by some schools, could be consolidated in more reciprocal partnerships. This could be achieved by inviting parents, carers, and educational communities to work in alliance with schools in reforming the grammar of schooling in terms of pedagogical relations with local communities and co-production and co-design of projects and activities that benefit, and voice, all stakeholders.

Collaborations and exchange with other educational and community realities

Technologies can support a wide range of activities that enable exploration and reflection on real life outside the school, informing the curriculum in a decolonial way. Taking account of multiple geographies and cartographies of education, welcoming voices and experiences from around the world, and being informed by local knowledge can only enhance students' educational experiences. This could be done through face-to-face and virtual workshops, to stimulate connections, collaborations, and discussions that can inform school curricula and teachers' pedagogies.

Unsettling identities for a socially just education?

The COVID-19 pandemic threw significant challenges at all those involved in education – students and their parents and carers, teachers and school leaders, and educational communities – requiring all to respond and adapt quickly and swiftly. They did. Notwithstanding some of the new exclusions that arose from the rapid uptake of technologies and the poverty related disadvantages that affected some, there was a phenomenal degree of resourcefulness, creativity, and capability, and we have documented some of this in the book.

The pandemic has also provided a moment to pause and reflect and to question the kind of educational practices that we learned to put up with as part of what was "normal" and ponder whether we want to go on with these. Through both our study and this book we have sought to expose some of the exclusionary rationales and ways of thinking, doing, and making intelligible education practices and subjects that the pandemic reiterated through the use of technologies. Yet, our intent was also to make visible school communities and to voice children's, families', teachers', and leaders' reckonings for an "ethics of possibility" (Appadurai, 2013, p. 295). This encompasses ways of thinking, feeling, and acting that broaden the horizons of what is possible and is thus a hopeful orientation which recognises people's role as "future makers" (Appadurai, 2013, p. 285). The ethics of possibility is the antithesis, or the antidote, to the "ethics of probability" (Appadurai, 2013, p. 295), the incessant calculation of us and our place in the world, which has created a malaise in our society (Baudrillard, 1985).

If, during the pandemic, the swift turn to distance teaching and learning mediated by digital technologies produced new forms of marginalisations and exclusions, this ethics of possibility has a great potential to be expanded and enriched through encounters with digital and non-digital technologies. In this book we attempted to show how these encounters can facilitate the concerted efforts of educational communities to challenge "historical injustices" and foster "cultural resilience to overcome injustice" (Ladson-Billings, 2021, p. 76). It is these concerted and critical efforts that can expand the possibilities for subjective experiences (Santos, 2018) but also allow a cross-fertilisation of practices and epistemologies (Connell, 2011; Peruzzo, 2021) that does not retreat to, or attempt to recapture, the grammar of schooling. Therefore, the COVID-19 pandemic, despite bringing global disruptions, made visible a future that is full of possibilities and invitations to new ways of doing, of being, and of becoming. Teachers, school leaders, families, children, and young people and educational communities showed us the way to more socially just, equitable and inclusive forms of schooling and education, using technologies in ways that are meaningful, respectful, and participated in across local and global scales.

References

Allan, J. (2006). The repetition of exclusion. *International Journal of Inclusive Education*, 10 (2–3), pp. 121–134.

Allan, J. (2008). *Rethinking inclusive education: The philosophers of difference in practice*. Dordrecht: Springer.

Allan, J. and Harwood, V. (2022). *On the self: Discourses of mental health and education*. Basingstoke: Palgrave Macmillan.

Annamma, S., Connor, D. and Ferri, B. (2016). Dis/ability critical race studies (DisCrit): Theorizing at the intersections of race and dis/ability. In: D. Connor, B. Ferri and S. Annamma, eds., *DisCrit: Disability studies and critical race theory in education*. New York: Teachers College Press, pp. 9–32.

Appadurai, A. (2013). *The future as cultural fact: Essays on the global condition*. London: Verso.

Apple, M. and Teitelbaum, K. (2001). John Dewey 1859–1952. In: J. A. Palmer, ed., *Fifty major thinkers on education: From Confucius to Dewey*. London and New York: Routledge, pp. 177–181.

Arendt, H. (2006). *Between past and future: Eight exercises in political thought*. London: Penguin Books.

Armstrong, D. (2003). *Experiences of special education: Re-evaluating policy and practice through life stories*. London: Routledge.

Armstrong, A., Armstrong, D. and Spandagou, I. (2010). *Inclusive education: International policy and practice*. London: SAGE.

Arnot, M. (1983). A cloud over coeducation: An analysis of the forms of transmission of class and gender relations. In: S. Walker and L. Barton, eds., *Gender, class, and education*. New York: Falmer Press, pp. 69–92.

Artiles, A. and Trent, S. C. (1994). Overrepresentation of minority students in special education: A continuing debate. *Journal of Special Education,* 27(4), pp. 410–437.

Baglieri, S. and Llavani, P. (2020). *Undoing ableism – Teaching about disability in K-12 classrooms.* New York/Abingdon: Routledge.

Ball, S. J. (2007). *Education plc: Understanding private sector participation in public sector education.* Abingdon and New York: Routledge.

Ball, S. J. (2010). The necessity and violence of theory. In: P. Thomson and M. Walker, eds., *The Routledge doctoral student's companion. Getting to grips with research in education and the social sciences.* 1st edition. London and New York: Routledge, pp. 67–75.

Ball, S. J. (2012). *Global Education Inc. New policy networks and the neo-liberal imaginaries.* London and New York: Routledge.

Ball, S. J. (2013). *Foucault, power and education.* London: Routledge.

Ball, S. J. (2021). *The education debate.* 3rd edition. London: Routledge.

Ball, S. J. and Collet-Sabé, J. (2021). Against school: A sociological critique. *Discourse: Studies in the cultural politics of education, online first.* https://doi.org/10.1080/01596306.2021.1947780.

Ball, S. J., Macguire, M. and Braun, A., with Hoskins, D. and Perryman, J. (2012). *How schools do policy.* London: Routledge.

Bardosh, K., Vries, D. de, Stellmach, D., Thorlie, A., Cremers, L. and Kinsman, J. (2019). *Towards people-centred epidemic preparedness & response: From knowledge to action.* London: Wellcome Trust.

Baudrillard, J. (1985). The masses: The implosion of the social in the media. *New Literary History,* 16(3), pp. 577–589.

Bello, A. (2021). How test publishers are poised to profit from pandemic 'learning loss'. *Forbes,* April 7. [Online] Available at: www.forbes.com/sites/akilbello/2021/04/07/how-test-publishers-are-poised-to-profit-from-pandemic-learning-loss/ [Accessed 9 Nov. 2022].

Benn, C. (1982). The myth of giftedness (Part II). *FORUM*, 24(3), pp. 83–84.

Benn, M. and Martin, J. (2018). The 'patron saint' of comprehensive education': An interview with Clyde Chitty. Part Two. *FORUM*, 60(1), pp. 11–30.

Bernstein, R. (2010). Dewey's vision of radical democracy. In: M. Cochrane, ed., *The Cambridge companion to Dewey*. Cambridge: Cambridge University Press, pp. 288–308.

Berliner, D. C. and Biddle, B. J. (2001). Thinking about education in a different way. In: *The Jossey Bass reader on school reform*. San Francisco: Jossey Bass, pp. 407–418.

Biesta, G. J. J. (2006). "Of all affairs, communication is the most wonderful:" Education as communicative praxis. In: D. T. Hansen ed., *John Dewey and our educational prospect: A critical engagement with Dewey's democracy and education*. Albany, NY: SUNY Press, pp. 23–37.

Biesta, G. J. J. (2014). Pragmatising the curriculum: Bringing knowledge back into the curriculum conversation, but via pragmatism. *The Curriculum Journal*, 25(1), pp. 29–49.

Biesta, G. J. J. and Miedena, S. (2000). Context and interaction: How to assess Dewey's influence on educational reform in Europe. *Studies in Philosophy and Education,* 19, pp. 21–37.

Biesta, G. J. J. and Burbules, N. (2003). *Pragmatism and educational research*. Lanham, MD: Rowman and Littlefield.

Blundell, R., Costa Dias, M., Joyce, R. and Xu, X. (2020). *COVID-19 and inequalities*. London: Institute for Fiscal Studies.

Booth, T. (2003). Views from the institution: Overcoming barriers to inclusive teacher education? In: T. Booth, K. Nes and M. Strømstad, eds., *Developing inclusive teacher education*. London: RoutledgeFalmer, 33–58.

Bourassa, G. (2021). Neoliberal multiculturalism and productive inclusion: Beyond the politics of fulfillment in education. *Journal of Education Policy*, 36(2), pp. 253–278.

Brah, A. (1996). *Cartographies of diaspora: Contesting identities*. London and New York: Routledge.

Brah, A. and Phoenix, A. (2004). Ain't I a woman? Revisiting intersectionality. *Journal of International Women's Studies*, 5(3), pp. 75–86.

Bruno-Jofré, R. and Schriewer, J. (2012). *The global reception of John Dewey's thought: Multiple refractions through time and space*. New York and London: Routledge.

Bradley, N. (2021). *'Locked out': Digital disadvantage of disabled children, young people and families during the COVID-19 pandemic*. London: KIDS. [Online] Available at: www.kids.org.uk/Handlers/Download.ashx?IDMF=15efa79c-daa9-45a3-84a8-7dc21d38f8a3 [Accessed 9 Nov. 2022].

Brantlinger, E. (2006). The big glossies: How textbooks structure (special) education. In: E. Brantlinger, ed., *Who benefits from special education? Remediating (fixing) other people's children*. Mahwah, New Jersey/London: Lawrence Erlbaum Associates, pp. 45–76.

Burrows, S. (2021). Researching learning loss: Findings from the first stage. *Renaissance blog*, February 24. [Online] Available at: www.renlearn.co.uk/renaissance-blog/researching-learning-loss-findings-from-the-first-stage/ [Accessed 9 Nov. 2022].

Carr, J. (2021). DfE laptop firm profits soar by nearly 50% to £207 m. *Schools Week*, March 16. [Online] Available at: https://schoolsweek.co.uk/dfe-laptop-firm-profits-soar-by-nearly-50-to-207m/ [Accessed 9 Nov. 2022]

Castañeda, L. and Williamson, B. (2021). Assembling new toolboxes of methods and theories for innovative critical research on educational technology. *Journal of New Approaches in Educational Research*. 10(1), pp. 1–14, https://doi.org/10.7821/naer.2021.1.703.

Chitty, C. (1979). Inside the secondary school: Problems and perspectives. In: D. Rubinstein, ed., *Education and equality*, Harmondsworth: Penguin, pp. 150–163.

Clarke, M. (2020). Eyes wide shut: The fantasies and disavowals of education policy. *Journal of Education Policy*, 35(2), pp. 151–167.

Cone, L., Brøgger, K., Berghmans, M., Decuypere, M., Förschler, A., Grimaldi, E., et al. (2021). Pandemic acceleration: Covid-19 and the emergency digitalization of European education. *European Educational Research Journal*, Online First, pp. 1–24.

Connell, R. (2011). 'Southern bodies and disability: Re-thinking concepts', *Third World Quarterly* 32(8), pp. 1369–81, doi: 10.1080/01436597.2011.614799.

Corona Showcase (2021). *Corona multimedia showcase: International celebration of creativity in the time of a pandemic*. [Online] Available at: https://coronashowcase.org/about-us/ [Accessed 9 Nov. 2022].

Cranmer, S. (2021). *Disabled children and digital technologies: learning in the context of inclusive education*. London: Bloomsbury Academic.

Cremin, L. A. (1991). *Popular education and its discontents*. New York: HarperCollins.

Cuban, L. (1986). *Teachers and machines: The classroom use of technology since 1920*. London: Teachers College Press.

Cuban, L. (2008). The perennial reform: Fixing school time. *Phi Delta Kappan*, 90(4), pp. 240–250.

Cuban, L. (2012). Why so many structural changes in schools and so little reform in teaching practice? *Journal of Educational Administration*, 51(2), pp. 109–125.

Cuban, L. (2020). Commentary: Reforming the grammar of schooling again and again. *American Journal of Education*, 126(4), pp. 665–671.

Cullimane, C. and Montacute, R. (2020). *Covid-19 impacts: Schools shutdown. Impact Brief #1 Social mobility.* London: Sutton Trust. [Online] Available at: www.suttontrust.com/our-research/covid-19-and-social-mobility-impact-brief/ [Accessed 2 Sept. 2022].

D'Alessio, S. (2011). *Inclusive education in Italy: A critical analysis of the policy of integrazione scolastica.* Rotterdam/Boston/Taipei: Sense Publishers.

Danforth, S., Taff, S. and Ferguson, P. M. (2008). Place, profession, and programme in the history of special education curriculum. In: E. A. Brantlinger, ed., *Who benefits from special education? Remediating (fixing) other people's children.* London: Lawrence Erlbaum Associates Publishers, pp.1–26.

Darling-Hammond, L. (2001). Inequality in teaching and schooling: How opportunity is rationed to students of color in America. In: Association of Academic Health Centers, C. H. Evans, Association of American Medical Colleges, L. Colburn, Institute of Medicine, A. Y. Stith and B. Smedley, eds., *The right thing to do, the smart thing to do: Enhancing diversity in health professions: Summary of the symposium on diversity in health professions in honor of Herbert W. Nickens M.D.* Washington DC: National Academies Press, pp. 208–233.

Decuypere, M., Grimaldi, E. and Landri, P. (2021). Introduction: Critical studies of digital education platforms, *Critical Studies in Education*, 62(1), pp. 1–16, doi:10.1080/17508487.2020.1866050.

Dahlberg, G., Moss, P. and Pence, A. (2007). *Beyond quality in early childhood education and care: Languages of evaluation.* 2nd edition. London: Routledge.

Deleuze, G. (1990). Postscript on the societies of control. *Pourparlers.* Paris: Editions Minuit.

Deleuze, G. (2004). *Difference and repetition.* London: Continuum.

Deleuze, G. and Guattari, F. (1987). *A thousand plateaus: Capitalism and schizophrenia.* London: The Athlone Press.

Deleuze, G. and Parnet, C. (1987). *Dialogues*. Trans. H. Tomlinson and B. Habberjam. New York: Columbia University Press.

Depaepe, M., Dams, K., de Vroede, M., Eggermont, B. Lauwers, H., Simon, H., Vandenberghe, R. and Verhoeven, J. (2000). *Order in progress: Everyday education practice in primary Schools – Belgium, 1880–1970*. Leuven: Leuven University Press.

Department for Education, (2019). *Permanent and fixed-period exclusions in England 2017–2018*. London: Department for Education. [Online] Available at: www.gov.uk/government/statistics/permanent-and-fixed-period-exclusions-in-england-2018-to-2019 [Accessed 9 Nov. 2022].

Derrida, J. (1992). Force of law: The mystical foundation of authority, trans. M. Quaintance. In: D. Cornell, M. Rosenfield and D. Carlson, eds., *Deconstruction and the possibility of justice*. New York and London: Routledge, pp. 3–67.

De Lissovoy, N. (2010). Decolonial pedagogy and the ethics of the global. *Discourse: Studies in the Cultural Politics of Education*, 31(3), pp. 279–293.

Dewey, J. (1899). *The school and society*. Chicago: University of Chicago Press.

Dewey, J. (1905). The postulate of immediate empricism. In: J. A. Boydston, ed., *The middle works (1899–1924), volume 3*. Carbondale and Edwardsville: Southern Illinois University Press, pp. 158–167.

Dewey, J. (1939). Experience, knowledge and value: A rejoinder. In: J. A. Boydston, ed., *The later works (1925–1953), volume 14*. Carbondale and Edwardsville: Southern Illinois University Press, pp. 3–90.

Dewey, J. (2014). *Ethical issues underlying education*. Miami: Hardpress Publishing.

Du Bois, W. E. B. (1920). Race intelligence. *The Crisis*, 20(3), pp. 117–120.

Du Bois, W. E. B. (1989). *The souls of black folk.* New York: Penguin Books. (Original work published 1904.)

Education Policy Institute. (2020a). *Understanding progress in the 2020/21 academic year: Complete findings from the autumn term.* [Online] Available at: https://assets.publishing.service.gov.uk/government/uploads/system/uploads/attachment_data/file/994350/Understanding_Progress_in_the_2020_21_Academic_Year_Report_2.pdf [Accessed 9 Nov. 2022].

Education Policy Institute. (2020b). *Understanding progress in the 2020/21 academic year: Initial findings from the spring term.* [Online] Available at: https://assets.publishing.service.gov.uk/government/uploads/system/uploads/attachment_data/file/994364/Understanding_Progress_in_the_2020_21_Academic_Year_Initial_Report_3_.pdf [Accessed 9 Nov. 2022].

Elliot, J. (2001). Characteristics of performative cultures: Their central paradoxes and limitations of educational reform. In: D. Gleeson and C. Husbands, eds., *The performing school.* London: Routledge, pp. 192–209.

Emdin, C., and Adjapong, E., eds. (2018). *#HipHopEd: The compilation on hip hop education* (Vol. 1). Rotterdam: Sense Publishers.

Erevelles, N. (2000). Educating unruly bodies: Critical pedagogy, disability studies and the politics of schooling. *Educational Theory,* 50(1), pp. 25–47.

Feenberg, A. (1991). *The critical theory of technology.* New York: Oxford University Press.

Ferguson, D. (2020). Boris Johnston's catch up tutoring 'will arrive too late' for pupils who need it most. *The Guardian,* 6 September. [Online] Available at: www.theguardian.com/education/2020/sep/06/boris-johnsons-catch-up-tutoring-will-arrive-too-late-for-pupils-who-need-it-most [Accessed 9 Nov. 2022].

Fielding, M., ed. (2001). *Taking education really seriously: Four years' hard labour.* London and New York: Routledge.

Fielding, M. and Moss, P. (2010). *Radical education and the common school*. Abingdon and New York: Routledge.

Foucault, M. (1972). *The archaeology of knowledge*. London: Tavistock Publications.

Foucault, M. (1977). *Discipline and punish: The birth of the prison*. New York: Vintage Books.

Foucault, M. (1991). Governmentality. In: G. Burchell, C. Gordon and P. Miller, eds., *The Foucault effect: Studies in governmentality, with two lectures by and an interview with Michel Foucault*. London: Harvester Wheatsheaf, pp. 87–104.

Foucault, M. (2004). *Society must be defended: Lectures at the College de France 1975–76*. London: Penguin books.

Foucault, M., (2005). *The order of things: An archaeology of the human sciences*. London and New York: Routledge Classics.

Foucault, M. (2008). *The birth of biopolitics: Lectures at the College de France, 1978–1979*. Basingstoke: Palgrave Macmillan.

Fukuyama, F. (2001). Social capital, civil society and development. *Third World Quarterly,* 22(1), pp. 7–20.

Garg, S., Kim, L., and Whitaker, M. (2020). Hospitalization rates and characteristics of patients hospitalized with laboratory-confirmed *Coronavirus Disease* 2019—COVID-NET, 14 States, March 1–30, 2020. Morbidity and Mortality Weekly Report, 69(15), pp. 458–464.

Gewirtz, S., Ball, S. and Bowe, R. (1995). *Markets, choice and equity in education*. Buckingham: Open University Press.

Giannini, S. and Grant Lewis, S. (2020). Three ways to plan for equity during the coronavirus school closures, *World Education Blog*, March 25. [Online] Available at: www.iiep.unesco.org/en/three-ways-plan-equity-during-coronavirus-school-closures-13365 [Accessed 9 Nov. 2022].

Giannini, S. 2020. *Come together, now!* [Online] Available at: https://en.unesco.org/voices/covid19_unprecedent_education_emergency [Accessed 9 Nov. 2022].

Gillborn, D. (2019). Hiding in plain sight: Understanding and addressing whiteness and color-blind ideology in education. *Kappa Delta Pi Record,* 55(3), pp. 112–117.

Gillborn, D. (2010). Reform, racism and the centrality of whiteness: Assessment, ability and the 'new eugenics', *Irish Educational Studies*, 29(3), pp. 231–252, doi:10.1080/03323315.2010.498280.

Global Partnership for Education. (2020). Inclusive education in a post-covid world: New report from humanity and inclusion. [Online] Available at: www.globalpartnership.org/blog/inclusive-education-post-covid-world-new-report-humanity-inclusion [Accessed 9 Nov. 2022].

Good Law Project. (2021). Firm founded by Tory Donor providing substandard laptops for vulnerable children. *Good Law Project*, January 24. [Online] Available at: https://goodlawproject.org/update/computacenter-laptops/ [Accessed 9 Nov. 2022].

Gorski, P. (2005). Education equity and the digital divide. *AACE Journal,* 13(1), pp. 3–45.

Gourlay, L., Littlejohn, A., Oliver, M. and Potter, J. (2021). Lockdown literacies and semiotic assemblages: Academic boundary work in the Covid-19 crisis. *Learning, Media and Technology*, 46(4), pp. 377–389.

GOV.UK. (2019). *Guidance: Children of critical workers and vulnerable children who can access schools or educational settings.* [Online] Available at: www.gov.uk/government/publications/coronavirus-covid-19-maintaining-educational-provision/guidance-for-schools-colleges-and-local-authorities-on-maintaining-educational-provision (withdrawn on 1 April 2022) [Accessed 9 Nov. 2022].

GOV.UK (2021) *"Pupils' progress in the 2020 to 2021 academic year: Interim report".* Gov.uk, February 24. [Online] Available at: www.

gov.uk/government/publications/pupils-progress-in-the-2020-to-2022-academic-years [Accessed 9 Nov. 2022].

Grek, S., and Landri, P. (2021). Editorial: Education in Europe and the COVID-19 pandemic. *European Educational Research Journal* 20(4), pp. 393–402. doi:10.1177/14749041211024781.

Grossberg, I. (1997) *Bringing it all back home: Essays on cultural studies.* Durham, NC: Duke University Press.

Hacking, I. (1991). How should we do the history of statistics? In: G. Burchell, C. Gordon, P. Miller, eds. *The Foucault effect: Studies in governmentality: With two lectures by and an interview with Michel Foucault.* Chicago: University of Chicago Press, pp. 181–196.

Harmey, S., and Moss, G. (2021). Learning disruption or learning loss: Using evidence from unplanned closures to inform returning to school after COVID-19, *Educational Review*, Online first. doi: 10.1080/00131911.2021.1966389.

Harry, B. and Klinger, J. (2014). *Why are so many minority students in special education?* New York: Teachers College Press.

Held, V. (2005). *The ethics of care: Personal, political and global.* Oxford: Oxford University Press.

Heller, R. (2020). What counts as a good school? A conversation with Larry Cuban. *Kappan,* 102(3), pp. 32–35.

Herenkohl, T., Scott, D., Higgins, D. J., Klika, J. B. and Lonn, B. (2021). How COVID-19 is placing vulnerable children at risk and why we need a different approach to child welfare. *Child Maltreatment*, 26(1), pp. 9–16.

Hickey-Moody, A. (2009). Becoming-dinosaur. Collective process and movement aesthetics. In: L. Cull, ed., *Deleuze and performance.* Edinburgh: Edinburgh University Press, pp.161–180.

Hill, M. L. (2009). *Beats, rhymes, and classroom life: Hip hop pedagogy and the politics of identity.* London: Teachers College Press.

Hoffman, P. (2018). *Data violence and how bad engineering choices can damage society.* [Online] Available at: https://medium.com/s/story/data-violence-and-how-bad-engineering-choices-can-damage-society-39e44150e1d4 [Accessed 9 Nov. 2022].

Holt, J. C. (2017). *Freedom and beyond.* Medford, MA: HOLTGWS.

Hooks, B. (1994). *Teaching to transgress.* New York and Abingdon: Routledge.

Howard, J. (1998). 'Subjectivity and space: Deleuze and Guattari's BwO in the new world order.' In: E. Kaufman and K. J. Heller (eds), Deleuze and Guattari: *New Mappings in Politics, Philosophy and Culture,* Minneapolis/London: University of Minnesota Press.

Hunter, I. (1996). Assembling the school. In: A. Barry, T. Osborne, N. Rose, eds., *Foucault and political reason: Liberalism, neo-liberalism and rationalities of government.* London: UCL Press, pp. 143–166.

Illich, I. (2006). *Deschooling society.* London: Marian Boyers.

Illich, I. (2009). *Tools for conviviality.* London: Marian Boyers.

Johns, F. (2021). Governance by data. *Annual Review of Law and Social Science,* 17, pp. 53–71.

Kendall, G. and Winkham, G. M. (1999). *Using Foucault's methods.* London: SAGE Publications.

Kirp, D. L. (1979). The vagaries of discrimination: Busing, policy, and law in Britain, *The School Review,* 8 (3), pp. 269–294.

Kozol, J. (1991). *Savage inequalities: Children in America's schools.* New York: Crown.

Ladson-Billings, G. (2006). From the achievement gap to the education debt: Understanding achievement in U.S. schools. *Educational Researcher,* 36(7), pp. 3–12.

Ladson-Billings, G. (2021). I'm here for the hard re-set: Post pandemic pedagogy to preserve our culture. *Equity & Excellence in Education,* 54(1), pp. 68–78.

Levitas, R. (2008). Be realistic: demand the impossible. *New Formations,* 65, Autumn, pp. 78–93.

Lingard, B. (2014). *Politics, policies and pedagogies in education. The selected works of Bob Lingard.* Abingdon and New York: Routledge.

Lingard, B., Wyatt-Smith, C. and Heck, E. (2021). Transforming schooling through digital disruption: Big data, policy, teaching, and assessment. In: C. Wyatt-Smith, B. Lingard and E. Heck, eds., *Digital disruption in teaching and testing: Assessments, big data and the transformation of schooling.* New York and Abingdon: Routledge, pp. 1–33.

Loopstra, R. (2020). *COVID-19: Latest impact on food.* London: Food Foundation.

MacArthur Foundation. *Safety and justice challenge exchange,* post by Christopher James (Mar. 4, 2021) [Online] Available at: https://safetyandjusticechallenge.org/blog/exploring-the-difference-between-racial-equality-and-racial-equity/ [Accessed 9 Nov. 2022].

McDermott, R. P. (1993). The acquisition of a child by a learning disability. In: C. Chaiklin and J. Lave, eds., *Understanding practice: Perspectives on activity and context.* New York: Cambridge University Press, pp. 269–305.

McGeehan, P. (2020). They're still working at airports, and they're scared. *New York Times.* [Online] Available at: www.nytimes.com/2020/04/28/nyregion/coronavirus-nyc-airports-workers.html [Accessed 9 Nov. 2022].

Macgilchrist, F., Allert, H. and Bruch, A. (2020). Students and society in the 2020s. Three future 'histories' of education and technology, *Learning, Media and Technology,* 45(1), pp. 76–89.

Macgilchrist, F. (2021). What is 'critical' in critical studies of edtech? Three responses, *Learning, Media and Technology,* 46(3), pp. 243–249.

Malaguzzi, L. (1996). *The hundred languages of children: The Reggio Emilia approach to early childhood education.* New Jersey: Ablex Publishing Corporation.

Manolev, J., Sullivan, A. and Slee, R. (2019). The datafication of discipline: ClassDojo, surveillance and a performative classroom culture. *Learning, Media and Technology,* 44(1), pp. 36–51.

Martin, J. (2015). Building comprehensive education: Caroline Benn and Holland Park School. *FORUM,* 57(3), pp. 363–386.

Matthews-Burwell, V. (1994). Drinking it all in, *New York Times,* February 12, p. 15.

Mignolo, W. (2011). *The Darker Side of Western Modernity: Global Futures, Decolonial Options.* Durham, NC: Duke University Press.

Mollicchi, S., Peppin, A., Safak, C. and Walker, T. (2020). Pandemics, power, and publics: Trends in post-crisis health technology. In: L. Taylor, G. Sharmi, A. Martin and S. Jameson, eds., *Data justice and Covid-19: Global perspectives.* London: Meatspace Press, pp. 276–283.

Murphy, R., Roschelle, J., Feng, M. and Mason, C. (2020). Investigating efficacy, moderators and mediators for an online mathematics homework intervention. *Journal of Research on Educational Effectiveness,* 13(2), pp. 235–270.

National Commission on Excellence in Education. (1983). *A nation at risk: the imperative for educational reform.* Washington: NCEE.

Nguyen, X. T. (2019). Unsettling 'inclusion' in the Global South: A post-colonial and intersectional approach to disability, gender, and education. In: M. J. Schuelka, C. J. Johnstone, G. Thomas and A. J. Artiles, eds., *The Sage handbook of inclusion and diversity in education.* SAGE Publications Ltd, pp. 28–40.

Noble, S. (2018). *Algorithms of oppression. How search engines reinforce racism.* New York: New York University Press.

Noddings, N. (1998). Thoughts on Dewey's 'ethical principles underlying education'. *Elementary School Journal*, 98, pp. 479–488.

Noddings, N. (2010). Dewey's philosophy of education: A critique from the perspective of care theory. In: M. Cochrane, ed., *The Cambridge companion to Dewey*. Cambridge: Cambridge University Press, pp. 265–287.

OECD. (2020). *Education and COVID-19: Focusing on the long-term impact of school closures*. [Online] Available at: www.oecd.org/coronavirus/policy-responses/the-impact-of-covid-19-on-student-equity-and-inclusion-supporting-vulnerable-students-during-school-closures-and-school-re-openings-d593b5c8/ [Accessed 9 Nov. 2022].

Olssen, L. (2009). *Movement and experimentation in young children's learning: Deleuze and Guattari in early childhood education*. London and New York: Routledge.

Olssen, M. (2003). Invoking democracy: Foucault's conception (with insights from Hobbes). *Paper presented at the British Educational Research Conference*, Edinburgh.

Owen, W. F., Carmona, R. and Pomeroy, C. (2020). Failing another national stress test on health disparities. *JAMA*. https://doi.org/10.1001/jama.2020.6547.

Pandemic Play Project. (2022). The pandemic play project: Documenting kids' culture during Covid-19. *International Journal of Play*, 11(1), pp. 12–33. [Online]. Available at: https://pandemicplayproject.com/ [Accessed 9 Nov. 2022].

Pangrazio, L. and Sefton-Green, J. (2021). Digital rights, digital citizenship and digital literacy: What's the difference? *Journal of New Approaches in Educational Research*, 10(1), pp. 15–27.

Pedley, R. (1970). *The comprehensive school*. Harmondsworth: Penguin.

Peruzzo, F. (2021). A call to rethink the Global North university: Mobilising disabled students' experiences through the encounter of critical disability studies and epistemologies of the South. Special issue: Education and the production of inequalities: Dialogues from the Global South and North, *Journal of Sociology*, pp. 1–18. doi: 10.1177/14407833211029381.

Peruzzo, F. and Allan J. (2022). Rethinking inclusive (digital) education: Lessons from the pandemic to reconceptualise inclusion through convivial technologies. *Journal of Learning, Media and Technologies*. Online First https://doi.org/10.1080/17439884.2022.2131817

Peruzzo, F., Ball, S. J. and Grimaldi, E. (2022). Peopling the crowded education state: Heterarchical spaces, EdTech markets and new modes of governing during the Covid-19 pandemic. *International Journal of Educational Research*, 114, 102006, pp. 1–13.

Pidd, H. (2020). 'It's a basic equality issue': Home learning gap between state and private schools, *Guardian*, 19 June. [Online] Available at: www.theguardian.com/education/2020/jun/19/its-a-basic-equality-issue-home-learning-gap-between-state-and-private-schools [Accessed 9 Nov. 2022].

Qureshi, Z. *Tackling the inequality pandemic: Is there a cure?* Brookings (Nov. 17, 2020) [Online] Available at: www.brookings.edu/research/tackling-the-inequality-pandemic-is-there-a-cure/ [Accessed 9 Nov. 2022].

Rabinow, P., ed. (1984). *The Foucault Reader*. New York: Pantheon Books.

Ragnedda, M. and Muschert, G. W. (2018). *Theorizing digital divides*. London and New York: Routledge.

Rajchman, J. (2000). *The Deleuze connection*. Cambridge, MA and London: MIT Press.

Ravitch, D. (2001). Reformers, radicals and romantics. In: *The Jossey Bass reader on school reform*. San Francisco: Jossey Bass, pp. 43–88.

Reay, D. (2020). English Education in the time of coronavirus. *Forum,* 62(3), pp. 311–322. http://dx.doi.org/10.15730/forum.2020.62.3.311.

Reuge, N., Jenkins, R., Brossard, M., Soobrayan, B., Mizunoya, S., Ackers, J., Jones, L. and Taulo, W. G. (2021). Education response to COVID 19 pandemic, a special issue proposed by UNICEF: Editorial review. *International Journal of Educational Development,* 87, p. 102485.

Richardson, J. and Powell, J. (2011). *Comparing special education: Origins to contemporary paradoxes.* Stanford: Stanford University Press.

RISE. (undated). *RISE module: Equality vs equity.* [Online] Available at: https://risetowin.org/what-we-do/educate/resource-module/equality-vs-equity/index.html [Accessed 9 Nov. 2022].

Roberts, N. and Danechi, S. (2022). *Coronavirus and schools.* House of Commons Library. [Online] Available at: https://researchbriefings.files.parliament.uk/documents/CBP-8915/CBP-8915.pdf [Accessed 9 Nov. 2022].

Rose, N. (1999). *Governing the soul: the shaping of the private self.* London: Free Association.

Roy, K. (2003). *Teachers in nomadic spaces: Deleuze and curriculum.* New York: Peter Lang.

Roy, A. (2020). The pandemic is a portal. The Financial Times, 3 April. [Online] Available at: www.ft.com/content/10d8f5e8-74eb-11ea-95fe-fcd274e920ca [Accessed 9 Nov. 2022].

Sancho-Gil, J. M., Rivera-Vargas, P. and Miño-Puigcercós, R. (2020). Moving beyond the predictable failure of Ed-Tech initiatives, *Learning, Media and Technology,* 45(1), pp. 61–75, doi: 10.1080/17439884.2019.1666873.

Santos, B. de S. (2018). *The end of the cognitive empire. The coming of age of the epistemologies of the South.* Durham and London: Duke University Press.

Santos, B. de S. (2021). *Il futuro comincia ora. Le vene aperte del mondo*. Roma: Castelvecchi.

School of Barbiana. (1990). *Lettera ad una professoressa*. Firenze: Libreria Editrice Fiorentina.

Shalaby, C. (2017). *Troublemakers*. Lessons in freedom from young children at school. New York: The New Press.

Selwyn, N. (2013). Discourses of digital 'disruption' in education: A critical analysis. *Fifth International Roundtable on Discourse Analysis, City University Hong Kong, May 23–25, 2013*.

Selwyn, N. (2017). Digital inclusion: Can we transform education through technology? *Colección Políticas Públicas* 103–107. *X Conferencia Internacional Encuentros 2016, Universidad de Barcelona*.

Selwyn, N. (2019). What's the problem with learning analytics? *Journal of Learning Analytics*, 6(3), pp. 11–19. http://dx.doi.org/10.18608/jla.2019.63.3.

Selwyn, N. and Jandrić, P. (2020). Postdigital living in the age of Covid-19: Unsettling what we see as possible. *Postdigital Science and Education*, 2, pp. 989–1005.

Selwyn, N., Hillman T., Eynon, R., Ferreira, G., Knox, J., Macgilchrist, F. and Sancho-Gil, J. (2020). What's next for Ed-Tech? Critical hopes and concerns for the 2020s. *Learning, Media and Technology*, 45(1), pp. 1–6.

Simmons, M. and Masschelein, J. (2015). Inclusive education for exclusive pupils. A critical analysis of the government of the exceptional. In: S. Tremain, ed., *Foucault and the government of disability*, 2nd edition. Ann Arbor: The University of Michigan Press, pp. 208–228.

Slee, R. (2013). How do we make inclusive education happen when exclusion is a political predisposition? *International Journal of Inclusive Education*, 17(8), pp. 895–907.

Slee, R. (2019). Belonging in an age of exclusion. *International Journal of Inclusive Education*, 23(9), pp. 909–922.

Smith, D. (1998). The place of ethics in Deleuze's philosophy: Three questions of immanence. In: E Kaufman and K J Heller, eds., Deleuze and Guattari: *New mappings in politics, philosophy and culture*. Minneapolis/London: University of Minnesota Press.

Social Metrics Commission. (2020). *Poverty and Covid-19. A Report of the social metrics commission.* [Online] Available at: https://socialmetricscommission.org.uk/wp-content/uploads/2020/08/SMC-Poverty-and-Covid-Report.pdf [Accessed 9 Nov. 2022].

Southgate, E. (2021). Artificial intelligence and machine learning: A practical guide for teachers. In: C. Wyatt-Smith, B. Lingard and E. Heck, eds., *Digital disruption in teaching and testing: Assessments, big data and the transformation of schooling*. New York/Abingdon: Routledge, pp. 60–74.

Starr, D. Hayes and Gao, N. (2022) The digital divide in education. Fact sheet June 2022 *Public Policy Institute of California*. [Online] Available at: www.ppic.org/wp-content/uploads/the-digital-divide-in-education.pdf [Accessed 9 Nov. 2022].

Stein, J., Latour, B. and Schultz. (2019). A Conversation with Bruno Latour and Nikolaj Schultz: Reassembling the geo-social. *Theory, Culture and Society,* 36(7–8), pp. 215–230.

Strathern, M. (2000). The tyranny of transparency. *British Journal of Educational Research,* 26(3), pp. 309–321.

Teräs, M., Suoranta, J., Teräs, H. and Curcher, M. (2020). Post-Covid-19 education and education technology 'solutionism': A seller's market. *Postdigital Science and Education,* 2, pp. 863–878.

Thompson, P. (2020). *School scandals: Blowing the whistle on the corruption of education system*. Bristol: Policy Press/Bristol University Press.

Tomlinson, S. (1985). The expansion of special education. *Oxford Review of Education,* 11(2), pp. 157–165.

Tomlinson, S. (2012). The irresistible rise of the SEN industry. *Oxford Review of Education*, 38(3), pp. 267–286.

Tomlinson, S. (2021). A sociology of special and inclusive education: Insights from the UK, US, Germany and Finland. In: A. Köpfer, J. Powell and R. Zahnd, eds., *International handbook of inclusive education*. Cologne: Verlag Barbara Budrich, pp. 59–73.

Tyack, D. and Tobin, W. (1994). The "grammar" of schooling: Why has it been so difficult to change? *American Educational Research Journal,* 31(3), pp. 453–479.

Tyack, D and Cuban, L. (1995). *Tinkering toward utopia: A century of public school reform.* Cambridge, MA and London: Harvard University Press.

United Nations Convention on the Rights of the Child (2021). General comment No 25 on children's rights in the context of a digital environment. [Online] Available at: https://docstore.ohchr.org/SelfServices/FilesHandler.ashx?enc=6QkG1d%2fPPRiCAqhKb7yhsqlkirKQZLK2M58RF%2f5F0vEG%2bcAAx34gC78FwvnmZXGFUI9nJBDpKR1dfKekJxW2w7O [Accessed 9 Nov. 2022].

UNICEF (2020a). *COVID-19 resources for policymakers and front-line workers.* [Online] Available at: www.unicef.org/coronavirus/covid-19-resources-policymakers-front-line-workers [Accessed 9 Nov. 2022].

UNICEF (2020b). *Don't let children be the hidden victims of COVID-19 pandemic.* [Online] Available at: www.unicef.org/press-releases/dont-let-children-be-hidden-victims-covid-19-pandemic [Accessed 9 Nov. 2022].

UNICEF (2020c). *Guidance for Covid-19 prevention and control in schools: Supplemental content F: Accelerated learning as Covid-19 response.* [Online] Available at: www.unicef.org/lac/media/12486/file/F-Accelerated%20Education%20as%20COVID-19%20Response.pdf [Accessed 9 Nov. 2022].

UNICEF (2021). *COVID-19 and school closures: One year of education disruption.* [Online] Available at: https://data.unicef.org/wp-cont

ent/uploads/2021/03/COVID19-and-school-closures-report.pdf [Accessed 9 Nov. 2022].

Unger, R. M. (2004). *False necessity: Anti-necessitarian social theory in the service of radical democracy. 2nd Edition.* London: Verso.

United Nations Refugee Agency. *Accelerated Education.* [Online] Available at: www.unhcr.org/uk/accelerated-education-working-group.html [Accessed 9 Nov. 2022].

Uslaner, E. M. (2002). *The moral foundations of trust.* Cambridge: Cambridge University Press.

Watermeyer, R. P., Crick, T., Knight, C. and Goodall, J. (2021). COVID-19 and digital disruption in UK universities: Afflictions and affordances of emergency online migration. *Higher Education,* 81(3), pp. 623–641.

White, J. (2007). *What schools are for and why? (Impact paper No 14).* London: Philosophy of Education Society of Great Britain.

Wilby, P. (2020). New schools, same results. *The Guardian,* 26 July. [Online] Available at: www.guardian.co.uk/commentisfree/2010/jul/26/schools-new-names-same-results [Accessed 9 Nov. 2022].

Wilkinson, R. and Pickett, K. (2009). *The spirit level: Why equal societies almost always do better.* London and New York: Allen Lane.

Williamson, B. (2021). Education technology seizes a pandemic opening, *Current History,* 120(822), pp. 15–20. https://doi.org/10.1525/curh.2021.120.822.15.

Williamson, B. and Hogan, A. (2020). *Commercialisation and privatisation in/of education in the context of Covid-19.* Brussels: Education International.

Williamson, B., Macgilchrist, F. and Potter, J. (2021). Covid-19 controversies and critical research in digital education. *Learning, Media and Technology,* 46(2), pp. 117–127.

Wright, E. O. (2010). *Envisioning real utopias.* London: Verso.

Wyatt-Smith, C., Lingard, B., and Heck, E., eds., (2021). *Digital disruption in teaching and testing assessments, big data, and the transformation of schooling*. London and New York: Routledge.

Yancy, C. W. (2020). COVID-19 and African Americans. *JAMA*. https://doi.org/10.1001/jama.2020.6548.

Youdell, D. (2006). *Impossible bodies, impossible selves: Exclusions and student subjectivities*. Dordrecht: Springer.

Zhao, Y. (2020). Tofu Is Not Cheese: Rethinking education amid the COVID-19 pandemic. *ECNU Review of Education*, 3(2), pp. 189–203.

Zigler, E. (2003). Forty years of believing in magic is enough. *Social Policy Report*, 17(1), p. 10.

Žižek, S. (2021). *Panic 2. Chronicles of a time lost*. New York: Polity Press.

Zuboff, S. (2019). *Il capitalismo della sorveglianza*. Luiss: University Press.

Index

affect 82, 87

Allan, Julie 4, 20, 36, 47, 49, 98

alliance 119

Arendt, Hannah 3, 109

assessment 9, 23, 30, 42, 53, 55, 59, 118

attainment 21, 39

Australia 5, 48

Ball, Stephen 16–17, 23, 28, 31, 51, 53, 56, 59, 71–73, 75, 105, 110

Barbiana 32

becomings 80, 82, 93, 107–108, 116

black 17, 19, 21–23, 25, 32, 38

categorisation 10, 22, 33–34, 68

children 1–4, 7, 10, 13–14, 18, 20–21, 24–25, 27, 29, 31, 33–35, 38–39, 44–46, 49–50, 52–55, 58–59, 61, 63–64, 66–70, 73, 75, 77–79, 81–85, 88–89, 91, 93, 96, 99–100, 102–104, 106–107, 109–118, 120–121

Chile 5, 81, 84

class 2, 12, 23, 31–32, 39, 45–46, 48, 53, 57, 59, 67, 73–75, 91, 101, 105, 118

collaborations 119

Collet-Sabé, Jordi 3, 10, 29–30, 32, 49, 75

communities 5, 25, 60, 68, 71, 77, 88, 90, 92, 94, 106, 109–110, 113–115, 117–121

community 13, 41, 69, 85, 89–91, 99, 109, 112, 114–116, 119

comprehensive schools 69

connections 7, 90–93, 99, 112, 119

conviviality 15, 75

Coronavirus *see* COVID-19

COVID-19 1, 3–5, 16, 19, 22–23, 25, 35, 59–60, 119, 121

crisis 2–4, 59, 69, 93, 97, 105

Cuban, Larry 27, 35, 37, 58, 64–65, 68, 70, 72

curriculum 6–7, 11, 30, 33, 44–45, 47, 63, 65–66, 69, 77, 83–84, 86–88, 90, 103, 107, 109, 114, 116, 118–119

Darling-Hammond, Linda 3, 21

De Lissovoy, Noah 5, 113

decolonial theory 6

decolonising 90, 106, 118

Deleuze, Gilles 6–8, 12, 32, 49, 52, 64, 77–80, 83, 92, 94, 107–108

Derrida, Jacques 19

deterritorialisation 6–8, 60, 64, 77, 83, 107

Dewey, John 64–66

digital 5, 13–14, 17, 24, 34–50, 53, 59, 64, 74, 81, 87, 97, 99, 101–102, 105–106, 109–118, 120

disadvantaged 1, 17, 19, 21, 23–25, 38, 68

disruption 11, 13, 33–34, 36, 59, 64, 88, 92, 97, 101, 121

edtech 41–42

England 5, 38, 40, 46, 49, 52, 54, 57, 83, 86, 90, 92, 95

Enlightenment period 28, 33, 58

epistemic 6, 28–29, 36, 39–40, 43, 49, 51, 58–60, 105–106

equality 11, 18–20, 68–69

equity 8, 11, 15, 18–19, 26, 29, 64, 92

ethics 15, 60, 65, 74, 120

exclusion 4, 10, 21, 31, 34, 43, 51, 57, 97, 103, 105

experimentation 118

families 52

flexibility 56, 115–116

Foucault, Michel 5, 28, 31, 33, 51, 56, 105

Global North 5, 28–29, 43, 58, 86–87, 99–100, 106, 113

Global South 5

grammar of schooling 4, 6–8, 26–29, 34–38, 40, 43–46, 48–49, 51–53, 55, 57–59, 61, 63–65, 67, 70, 72, 76, 78–79, 82–83, 87–88, 93, 100, 102, 104–108, 115–117, 119, 121

hierarchy 7, 29, 33, 36, 38, 44, 46, 49, 52, 55, 58–59, 77, 79, 83, 88, 93, 103, 106–107, 113, 115–116

identities 4–5, 45, 49, 77, 87, 95–96, 119

Illich, Ivan 14–16, 27, 75, 112

inclusion 14, 20, 36, 41, 49–50, 52–55, 58, 75, 95, 102, 113

indigenous 19, 33, 84–86, 90, 104

inequalities 17, 75

insider rewritings 77

Internet 17, 21

Italy 5, 32, 40, 44, 89–90, 95

judgement 33, 56

knowledge 4, 6–7, 17, 25–26, 28, 34–36, 58, 63, 66, 78, 83, 85–86, 91, 95, 99, 111, 115–116, 119

Ladson-Billings, Gloria 3, 21, 23, 25–26, 74, 76, 100, 121

leaders 5, 8, 11, 37, 63, 65, 76–77, 88, 93, 96, 98–100, 103, 108–110, 114–117, 120–121

learning 2, 7–9, 15–16, 20, 24–26, 29, 33–35, 38–39, 41–42, 44, 46–48, 50, 52–53, 57–58, 60, 63, 65, 72, 77–84, 86, 89–90, 93, 99–103, 109–118, 120

learning loss 9, 25

lines of flight 6, 8, 26, 64

lived experiences 4–5, 7, 63, 76–77, 96, 98, 104

low-income families 23, 68

Malaguzzi, Loris 63, 93

Malaysia 5, 78–80, 96, 98

Martin, Jane 67, 69

medicalising 48, 56, 112

micro-exclusions 44

Mignolo, Walter 5, 29

minority ethnic groups 3, 23

modernity 28, 106

normal 23, 25, 32, 34, 43, 84, 94, 100, 120

normalisation 10, 31, 36, 49, 58

observation 33–34, 53, 55

online 2, 5, 17, 38, 42, 44, 46, 48, 50, 52, 54, 57, 59, 77, 82, 91, 102

oppression 5–6, 23, 38, 87

pandemic 1–5, 8, 10, 16, 19–20, 22–25, 34–35, 37–41, 43, 57, 59–60, 63, 75, 78, 83, 88–91, 93, 96–98, 100–101, 103, 105–106, 109–110, 112–113, 115, 117, 119–120

parents 8, 49, 52–54, 63, 71, 73, 88–90, 92, 103, 117, 119–120

partnership 119

pedagogy 46–47, 59, 66, 82, 111

Peruzzo, Francesca 16–17, 36, 98, 121

power 5–6, 27–29, 31, 36, 38, 43–44, 49, 51–52, 54, 56, 58–60, 65, 75, 88, 91–92, 103, 105, 107–108, 117

professionals 4, 26, 52, 55, 76–77, 83, 87, 91, 93, 96, 104, 106

race 19, 21, 31, 33, 59, 74–75, 80, 101, 105, 114

racism 21, 51

Reay, Diane 10, 23–24, 39, 75

reform 64, 66, 69, 71–76, 93, 100, 117

repetition 27

rhizome 6–7, 64, 80, 107

Rose, Nikolas 31, 33, 56

Santos, Boaventura de Sousa 5–6, 29, 99, 106, 121

school closures 2, 24

schooling 9, 27

schools 2, 7–8, 10–11, 13, 16–17, 21, 23–25, 27–28, 32–34, 38–40, 42–43, 51, 57–58, 60, 62–63, 65, 67–73, 75, 79, 83, 86, 88, 92, 102, 106, 110, 117–119

smoothing 60, 63, 77, 83, 87, 103, 107, 115

socially just 3, 25–26, 95, 99, 115, 118–119, 121

space 4–5, 12, 21, 30, 39, 41, 47, 54, 56, 63, 65, 83–84, 87–88, 93, 97, 107, 115–117

special needs 17, 19–20, 25, 32, 80

student 3, 7, 13, 15, 21, 29, 31, 35, 44, 48–49, 80, 89

subjectivities 6, 13, 36, 43, 45, 52, 82, 87, 93, 101, 104, 107, 116

sustainable 108

teachers 5–8, 10–12, 16, 20–21, 26, 28, 34–37, 44, 49, 56, 63, 76, 78–80, 82–84, 87–89, 92–93, 96, 98–101, 103–104, 107–111, 114–120

technologies 5, 8, 12–17, 24, 34–37, 39–41, 43–44, 51–52, 54–55, 57, 59–60, 64, 75, 81, 87, 91, 95, 97, 99, 101–102, 106, 109–118, 120

territory 90

Tobin, William 4, 27–28, 49, 60, 63

Tomlinson, Sally 20, 23, 47

Tyack, David 4, 27–28, 49, 60, 63, 68, 70

UNICEF 1–2, 10, 21, 38, 43

US 5

virtual 38, 44, 53, 90, 101, 119

voice 111, 119–120

vulnerabilities 19, 22, 36–38, 40, 44, 50, 54, 59, 101, 103

Western 29, 34, 40, 49

Williamson, Ben 9, 14, 16, 34, 36–37, 39, 41, 43, 60

Zhao, Yong 4, 27, 36

Žižek, Slavoj 1, 12

www.ingramcontent.com/pod-product-compliance
Lightning Source LLC
Chambersburg PA
CBHW070808230426
43665CB00017B/2532